Hiking & Biking
Lake County, Illinois

An American Bike Trails Publication

Hiking & Biking
Lake County, Illinois

Published by   American Bike Trails
610 Hillside Avenue
Antioch, IL 60002

Created by   Ray Hoven
Designed by   Mary C. Rumpsa

Table of Contents

Table of Contents (continued)

Events & Programs – Lake County Forest Preserves

Acknowledgements

We appreciate the input and guidance of the many professionals who supported us in the development of this book, especially:

Susan Hawkins and Keith Portman - Lake County Forest Preserves

Bruce Christenson – Lake County Division of Transportation

Steve Bartram – Lake Forest Open Lands Association

Steven McLevich - Libertyville Parks Dept

Greg Behm - Volo Bog State Natural Area

Brent Kastor – Village of Vernon Hills

Nancy DeMuro and Frank Nickels – College of Lake County

The maps included are derived from source maps provided courtesy of the Lake County Forest Preserves, Lake County Division of Transportation, Friends of the Volo Bog, Heller Interpretive Center, Libertyville Parks Dept., and the Vernon Hills Parks District.

Introduction

Why not set aside the stresses and pressures around you for a while and visit one of Lake County's nearby parks or preserves. Spend just an hour or even a full day walking, biking or just relaxing. The woods, lakes, rivers, prairies, and savannas provide peaceful environments that can help you reflect and put things into perspective.

This book provides a comprehensive easy-to-use reference to the trail systems throughout Lake County, Illinois. It contains 34 maps representing over 260 miles of trail (exclusive of the Grand Illinois Trail). The trail systems are listed alphabetically, and there is an overview map of Lake County. Each trail map and description includes such helpful features as location and access, trail facilities and nearby communities.

The special sections included with this book are meant to provide a better understanding and appreciation of the environment around us, and the organizations that support it.

Lake County Forest Preserves
Describes the history, status and objectives of the Lake County Forest Preserves.

Definition of Terms

Defines terms commonly referred to when describing an geographic area or plant, such as prairie, savanna or herb.

Mammals of the Des Plaines River Valley

Lists the species, their common and scientific names, and their habitat. As an example the Mink (mustela vison) is most often found near streams and lakes.

Endangered Plants and Animals in Lake County

This listing provides both the common and scientific names of those plants and animals classified as endangered within Lake County, such as the Bearded Wheat Grass (agropyron subsecundum) and the Sandhill Crane (grus canadensis).

Health Hazards related to outdoor activities

Describes the symptoms and treatment of Hypothermia, Frostbite, Heat Stroke and the West Nile Virus.

Rules of the Trails

Rules common to trail and preserve use, and those specific to the Lake County's Forest Preserves and to Bicyclists.

Events and Programs – Lake County Forest Preserves

Lists many of the popular programs that have been made available through the Forest Preserves.

Organizations

Listings, with addresses and phone numbers, of Hiking, Environmental, Photography organizations, plus Lake County's Bicycle Stores.

Lake County Forest Preserves

The Lake County Forest Preserves manages nearly 25,000 acres of land and offers innovative educational, recreational and cultural opportunities for all ages. More than 50 endangered species take refuge in the Preserves, which boast some of Illinois' finest remaining natural areas, including the agency's 7,700-acre Des Plaines River Greenway. The Forest Preserves offer visitors nearly 112 miles of trail for a variety of outdoor recreation uses, fishing ponds and lakes, public access to the Fox River, award-winning nature and history education programs and events, and four public golf courses. Facilities of special interest include Independence Grove near Libertyville, the Lake County Discovery Museum near Wauconda, Greenbelt Cultural Center near Waukegan, the Fox River Forest Preserve near Barrington and Ryerson Conservation Area near Deerfield. Lake County's Forest Preserves roots reach back to 1957 and a three-year-old boy who wanted to go exploring in the woods. When Ethel Untermyer's son, Frank, made his request, she asked a friend where the nearest Forest Preserve was. Like many families, the Untermyers had just moved to Lake County from nearby Chicago and were unfamiliar with the area. She was stunned to hear Lake County had no Forest Preserves. So the next day, she did what few other 33-year-old homemakers would do. She organized a countywide referendum to create the Lake County Forest Preserve District. In those days, Lake County's population hadn't even reached 300,000. But people were already shaking their heads about the loss of open space. Unique to Illinois, forest preserve districts were designed to protect large natural areas. Education and recreation would be important offerings, but primarily within that natural context. Just four people came to Ethel's first meeting. She started driving her Studebaker throughout the county, frequently on dirt roads. She spoke with groups, sought out local leaders and got a quick education in politics. By election day in fall 1958, a groundswell of public support had emerged. The referendum passed with an overwhelming 60 percent of votes. Twenty days later, the Lake County Forest Preserve District was legally established in circuit court. A citizens' advisory committee was created, and Ethel Untermyer was named its chair. And in 1961, four years after Frank Untermyer asked for a place to explore, the first Lake County Forest Preserve was created: Van Patten Woods near Wadsworth. On that day, Ethel reflected on her efforts and said, "This is the secret, the magic everyone is looking for when they crave preservation of open areas: every solitary soul able to look beyond the end of his nose is the vital spark to achieving a Forest Preserve District. There is no apathy among the people." A 475-acre Preserve has been named "Ethel's Woods" in honor of her efforts to initiate the founding of the Lake County Forest Preserves. Ethel's Woods is located between Route 45 and Crawford Road, south of Route 173 near Old Mill Creek.

Take time to explore and enjoy the Lake County Forest Preserves throughout the year. For a free copy of LCFP's Horizons newsletter and Calendar of Events call 847-367-6640 or visit www.LCFPD.org.

Definition of Terms

Natural Community:

An indigenous group of organisms – interrelated with each other and their environment. Natural communities may be defined at any scale, from biome to micro association. Important characteristics include soil moisture, substrate, soil reaction, species composition, vegetation structure, and topographic position.

Prairie:

Grassland community in full sun dominated by a matrix of perennial grasses and supporting a diversity of forbs which forms a dry flammable turf. Prairies are essentially treeless, but shrubs may be present. Types range from wet to dry and include gravel hill, sand, dolomite bedrock and black soil prairies. Illinois is in the Tallgrass Prairie region.

Savanna:

Any area where scattered trees (usually oaks in Lake County) and/or shrubs occur over a continuous and permanent groundlayer, usually dominated by herbs. Savannas, considered fire-dependent grassland communities, range from dry (black oak savannas) to wet (swamp white oak savannas).

Woodland:

Community dominated in Lake County by a mix of oaks with understory trees. Moderately dense trees and shrubs (25-80% canopy) occurring over a continuous and permanent herbaceous groundlayer. A fire-dependent community which burned regularly if infrequently.

Forest:

Community dominated by maple with a dense canopy, more than 60-80%, and an understory vegetation not dominated by grasses. Characterized by multiple layers of shrubs, understory trees and canopy trees; shade tolerant herbaceous plants form the ground layer. In our area forests occur east of Lake Michigan and in ravines, floodplains and on the east side of large rivers. Forests are not fire-dependent communities although fires occasionally occurred.

Wetland:

Community or system having soils that are saturated, flooded or ponded long enough during the growing season to develop anaerobic conditions that favor the growth of hydrophytic vegetation (growing partially or wholly immersed in water). Wetlands include bogs, fens, marshes, swamps, interdunal swales, wet prairies, sedge meadows and woodland ponds.

Shrub:

Brushwood. A low, usually several-stemmed, woody plant.

Herb:

A seed producing annual, biennial, or perennial that does not develop persistent woody tissue but dies down at the end of a growing season.

Bog:

Wet, spongy ground. A poorly drained usually acid area rich in plant residues, frequently surrounding a boding of open water, and have a characteristic flora.

Fen:

Low land covered wholly or partly with water unless artificially drained.

Marsh:

A tract of soft wet land usually characterized by mono-cotyledons, such as grass or cattails.

Swale:

A lower lying or depressed and off wet stretch of land.

Sedge:

Turfed marsh plant having achene's and solid stems.

Mammals of Lake County's Des Plaines River Valley

SPECIES	HABITAT
Beaver (Castor)	streams, rivers, ponds, lakes
Eastern Chipmunk (Tamias striatus)	wooded and brushy areas
Eastern Cottontail (Sylvilagus floridanus)	woodlots and brushy areas
Eastern Fox Squirrel (Sciurus niger)	oak-hickory woodlands
Eastern Gray Squirrel (Sciurus carolinensis)	wooded areas
Grey Fox (Urocyon cinereoargenteus)	brushy and wooded areas
Longtail Weasel (Mustela frenata)	ubiquitous in terrestrial habitats
Masked Shrew) (Sorex cineereus)	prefers moist situations
Meadow Jumping Mouse (Zapus hudsonius)	meadows, fields, open woods
Meadow Vole) (Microtus pennsylvanicus)	fields, meadows, open woods
Mink (Mustela vison)	streams and lakes
Muskrat (Ondatra ziberthica)	marshes and sloughs
Raccoon (Procyon lotor)	wooded areas near water
Red Bat (Lasiurus borealis)	wooded areas, usually in old trees
Red Fox (Vulpes fulva)	brushy and wooded areas

eastern chipmunk

Mammals of Lake County's Des Plaines River Valley
(continued)

SPECIES	HABITAT
Shorttail Shrew (Blarina brevicauda)	ubiquitous in terrestrial situations
Southern Flying Squirrel (Glaucormys volans)	woodlands
Striped Skunk (Mephitis mephitis)	ubiquitous in terrestrialhabitats
13-lined Ground Squirrel (Citellus tridecemlineatus)	fields, meadows, open woods
White-footed Mouse (Peromyscus leucopus)	wooded or brushy areas
Whitetail Deer (Odocoileus virginianus)	wooded areas
Woodchuck (Marmota monax)	woodland edges, fields and meadows

Thirteen-lined Ground Squirrel

Endangered Plants in the Lake County Forest Preserves

COMMON NAME	SCIENTIFIC NAME
Autumn Willow	Salix serissima
Bearded Wheat Grass	Agropyron subsecundum
Brownish Sedge	Carex brunnescens
Buffaloberry	Sherpherdia Canadensis
Bunchberry	Cornus Canadensis
Common Bog Arrow Grass	Triglochin maritime
Cordroot Sedge	Carex chordorrhiza
Golden Sedge	Carex aurea
Grass Pink Orchid	Calopogon tuberosus
Grass-leaved Pondweed	Potamogeton gramineus
Hairy White Violet	Viola incognita
Highbush Blueberry	Vaccinium corymbosum
Jack Pine	Pinus banksiana
Kalm's St. John's Wort	Hypericum kalmianum
Large Cranberry	Vaccinium macrocarpon
Marram Grass	Ammophila breviligulata
Northern Cranesbill	Geranium bicknellii
Northern Gooseberry	Ribes hirtellum
Pitcher Plant	Sarracenia purpurea
Prairie White-fringed Orchid	Habenaria leucophaea
Pretty Sedge	Carex woodii
Purple Fringed Orchid	Plantathera psycodes
Round-leafed Sundew	Drosera rotundifolia
Rusty Cotton Grass	Eriophorum virginicum
Shadbush	Amelanchier interior
Showy Lady's Slipper	Cypripedium reginae
Slender Bog Arrow Grass	Triglochin palustris

Endangered Plants in the Lake County Forest Preserves
(continued)

COMMON NAME	SCIENTIFIC NAME
Small Cranberry	Vaccinium oxycoccos
Small Sundrops	Oenothera perennis
Small Yellow Lady's Slipper	Cypripedium calceolus
Smith's Bulrush	Scirpus smithii
Snake-mouth	Pogonia ophioglossoides
Three-seeded Sedge	Carex trisperma
Tubercled Orchid	Platanthera flava var. herbiola
Tuckerman's Sedge	Carex tuckermani
Water Marigold	Bidens beckii
White Lady's Slipper	Cypripedium candidum
Yellow Birch	Betula alleghaniensis

sundrops

Endangered Animals in the Lake County Forest Preserves

COMMON NAME	SCIENTIFIC NAME
Iowa Darter	Etheostoma exile
Eastern Massasauga	Sistrurus catenatus
American Bittern	Botaurus lentiginosus
Black Tern	Chidonia Niger
Black-crowned Night Heron	Nycticoraz nycticorax
Cooper's Hawk	Accipiter copperii
Forster's Tern	Sterna forsteri
Henslow's Sparrow	Ammodramus henslowii
Least Bittern	Ixobryclus exilis
Peregrine Falcon	Falco peregrinus
Red-shouldered Hawk	Buteo lineatus
Sandhill Crane	Grus canadensis
Yellow-headed Blackbird	Xanthocephalus

heron

Health Hazards

Hypothermia

Hypothermia is a condition where the core body temperature falls below 90 degrees. This may cause death.

Mild hypothermia

1. Symptoms
   a. Pronounced shivering
   b. Loss of physical coordination
   c. Thinking becomes cloudy
2. Causes
   a. Cold, wet, loss of body heat, wind
3. Treatment
   a. Prevent further heat loss, get out of wet clothing and out of wind. Replace wet clothing with dry.
   b. Help body generate more heat. Refuel with high-energy foods and a hot drink, get moving around, light exercise, or external heat.

Severe hypothermia

1. Symptoms
   a. Shivering stops, pulse and respiration slows down, speech becomes incoherent.
2. Treatment
   a. Get help immediately.
   b. Don't give food or water.
   c. Don't try to rewarm the victim in the field.
   d. A buildup of toxic wastes and tactic acid accumulates in the blood in the body's extremities. Movement or rough handling will cause a flow of the blood from the extremities to the heart. This polluted blood can send the heart into ventricular fibrillations (heart attach). This may result in death.
   e. Wrap victim in several sleeping bags and insulate from the ground.

Frostbite

Symptoms of frostbite may include red skin with white blotches due to lack of circulation. Rewarm body part gently. Do not immerse in hot water or rub to restore circulation, as both will destroy skin cell.

Heat Exhaustion

Cool, pale, and moist skin, heavy sweating, headache, nausea, dizziness and vomiting. Body temperature nearly normal.

Treatment: Have victim lie in the coolest place available– on back with feet raised. Rub body gently with cool, wet cloth. Give person ½ glass of water every 15 minutes if conscious and can tolerate it. Call for emergency medical assistance.

Health Hazards
(continued)

Heat Stroke

Hot, red skin, shock or unconsciousness; high body temperature.

Treatment: Treat as a life-threatening emergency. Call for emergency medical assistance immediately. Cool victim by any means possible. Cool bath, pour cool water over body, or wrap wet sheets around body. Give nothing by mouth.

West Nile Virus

West Nile Virus is transmitted by certain types of mosquitoes. Most people infected with West Nile Virus won't develop symptoms. Some may become ill 3 to 15 days after being bitten.

Protect Yourself

Wear property clothing, use insect repellents and time your outdoor activities to reduce your risk of mosquito bites and other insect problems. Most backyard mosquito problems are caused by mosquitoes breeding in and around homes, not those from more natural areas.

Trail & Preserve Rules

- Leave nature as your find it for others to enjoy.
- Do not collect and remove any natural objects.
- Deposit litter in proper receptacles
- Stay on trails
- Be alert for cars or bicycles
- Don't feed the wildlife.
- Check for ticks when you're finished.
- Don't wear earphones. You can't hear a bicyclist coming.
- Relax, have fun, and enjoy!

Specifics for Lake County's Forest Preserves

- Park in lots only.
- Deposit litter in proper receptacles.
- Permits are required for horseback riding, youth campgrounds, model airplane field, and picnic shelters for groups of 25 or more. Call 847-367-6640 for details.
- Snowmobiles must be registered with the State of Illinois.
- Stay on designated trails and follow signs and Preserve and trail regulations.
- Hunting, collecting, firearms and fires are prohibited.

Trail & Preserve Rules
(continued)

- State fishing regulations apply.

- Leash and pick up after all pets. Four permit-only Dog Exercise Areas allow dogs off-leash. Call 847-367-6640 for details.

- Preserve hours are from 6:30 am until sunset, unless otherwise noted.

- Releasing captured animals, feeding or disturbing wildlife and picking or damaging plants is prohibited.

- For emergencies call 911. For non-emergency public safety issues call 847-549-5200

Specifics for Bicyclists

- Wear a helmet.

- Ride in single file.

- Be alert for loose gravel, debris, holes, or bumps on the trails.

- Keep both hands on your handlebars.

- Apply your brakes gradually to maintain control on loose gravel or soil.

- Cautiously pass hikers on the left. Call out "passing on the left".

- Be courteous to hikers or horseback rides on the trail. They have the right of way.

- Don't carry items or attach anything to your bicycle that might hinder your vision or control.

- Don't carry extra clothing where it can hand down and jam in a wheel.

Hiking & Biking Trail Summary

LOCATION	HIKING	BIKING	SURFACE
Buffalo Creek Forest Preserve	4.0	4.0	Crushed granite
Buffalo Grove Bike Paths	45.0	45.0	21 miles of asphalt paths & 24 miles of concrete walk
Chain O'Lakes Bike Path	3.0	3.0	Asphalt
Chain O'Lakes State Park	16.0	6.0	8 miles of crushed gravel with 2.5 miles of woodchip
Cuba Marsh	2.0	2.0	Crushed granite
Des Plaines Greenway Trail	31.0	31.0	Crushed granite
Fox River Preserve & Marina	2.0	2.0	Crushed granite
Grand Illinois Trail	475.0	475.0	Mixed
Grant Woods Forest Preserve	6.0	6.0	Crushed granite
Grassy Lake Forest Preserve	3.5	- -	Crushed granite
Greenbelt Forest Preserve	4.0	5.0	Crushed granite
Half Day Forest Preserve	1.0	1.0	Crushed granite
Illinois Beach State Park	12.0	8.0	Crushed gravel, woodchip, sand
Independence Grove	7.0	7.0	Asphalt, crushed granite
Lake Forest Preserves	12.0	- -	Dirt
Lakewood Forest Preserve	12.0	3.0	Crushed granite
Libertyville's Butler Lake Trail	3.0	3.0	Asphalt
Lyons Woods Forest Preserve	3.0	3.0	Crushed granite
McDonald Woods Forest Preserve	4.5	3.5	Crushed granite
Middlefork Savanna Forest Preserve	4.0	4.0	Crushed granite
Millennium Trail - Lakewood FP section	3.2	3.2	Crushed granite
Millennium Trail - Hawley Street section	3.0	3.0	Asphalt
North Shore Bike Path	8.0	8.0	Crushed gravel, asphalt
Old School Forest Preserve	7.5	6.0	Crushed gravel, 1.5 mile asphalt road lane
Robert McClory Bike Path	25.0	25.0	Asphalt, crushed gravel Wilmette to Lake Bluff
Rollins Savanna Forest Preserve	5.7	5.0	Crushed granite
Ryerson Conservation Area	6.0	- -	Crushed granite
Skokie Valley Trail	6.5	6.5	Asphalt
Van Patten Woods Forest Preserve	5.0	4.0	Crushed granite
Vernon Hills Trails	7.0	7.0	Asphalt
Volo Bog State Natural Area	3.3	- -	Woodchip, boardwalk
Walter Heller Interpretive Center	3.3	- -	Crushed gravel, woodchip
Zion's Bike Paths	6.5	6.5	Crushed gravel, asphalt, streets
Wright Woods Forest Preserve	4.0	4.0	Crushed granite

Lake County Map

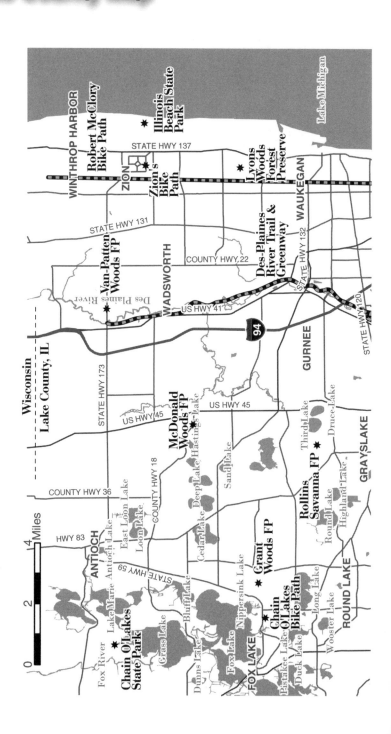

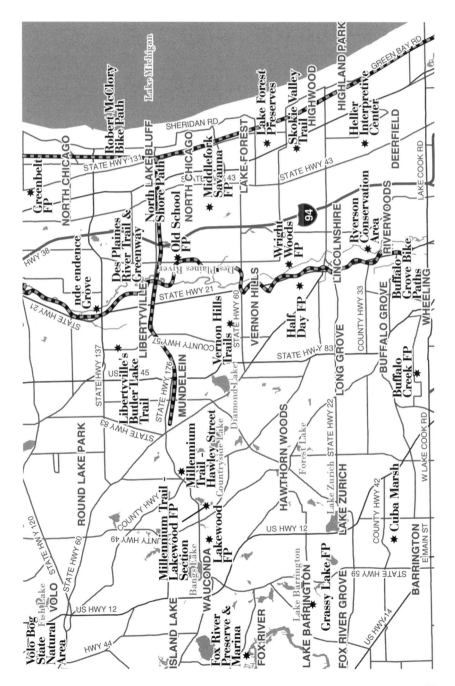

Explanation of Symbols

LEGEND

▬▭▬▭▬▭▬	Hiking/Biking Trail
▪ ▪ ▪ ▪ ▪ ▪	Hiking only Trail
▭▭▭▭▭▭	Alternate Trail
▸▪▸▪▸▪▸▪	Horseback/Snowmobile Trail
▪ ▪ ▪ ▪ ▪	Planned Trail
╫╫╫╫╫╫╫	Railroad Tracks

Facilities

▲	Camping
✚	First Aid
🍴	Food/Concession
ℹ	Information
🛏	Lodging
P	Parking
🪑	Picnic Area
👫	Rangers Station
🚻	Restroom
◤	Shelter
☎	Telephone
🚰	Water

SYMBOLS

 Wooded Area

 Preserve/City Boundary

 Rivers and Lakes

Buffalo Creek Forest Preserve

Set in the midst of the suburbs of Buffalo Grove, Arlington Heights, and Long Grove, the 387 acre Buffalo Creek Forest Preserve offers a quiet place to relax and reconnect with nature. A reservoir has been created, as a result of a dam built on Buffalo Creek for flood control. There are several small islands in the reservoir. Its design has created a natural-looking wetland. A diversity of grassland birds use the Preserve, including meadowlarks, bobolinks, pheasants, and cormorants.

There are 4 miles of crushed granite trails open to hikers, bicyclists and cross-country skiers. The entrance and parking area are located on Checker Road, just west of Arlington Heights Road. The main trailhead is at the Checker Road entrance. The trails generally run through open areas, crossing several creeks, skirting the reservoir and traversing restored prairie. There is drinking water, but there are no restroom facilities available. Signs along the trails describe the natural history of the area.

cormorant

Getting there:

Buffalo Creek is bordered on the south by Lake Cook Road, on the east by Arlington Heights Road, and on the north by Checker Road. Take Arlington Heights Road north and turn west on Checker Road. The entrance, with parking, is a short distance on the left. The preserve is open from 6:30 a.m. to sunset.

For more information:

Lake County Forest Preserves
www.LCFPD.org
2000 North Milwaukee Avenue
Libertyville, Illinois 60048
847-367-6640

Buffalo Creek Forest Preserve

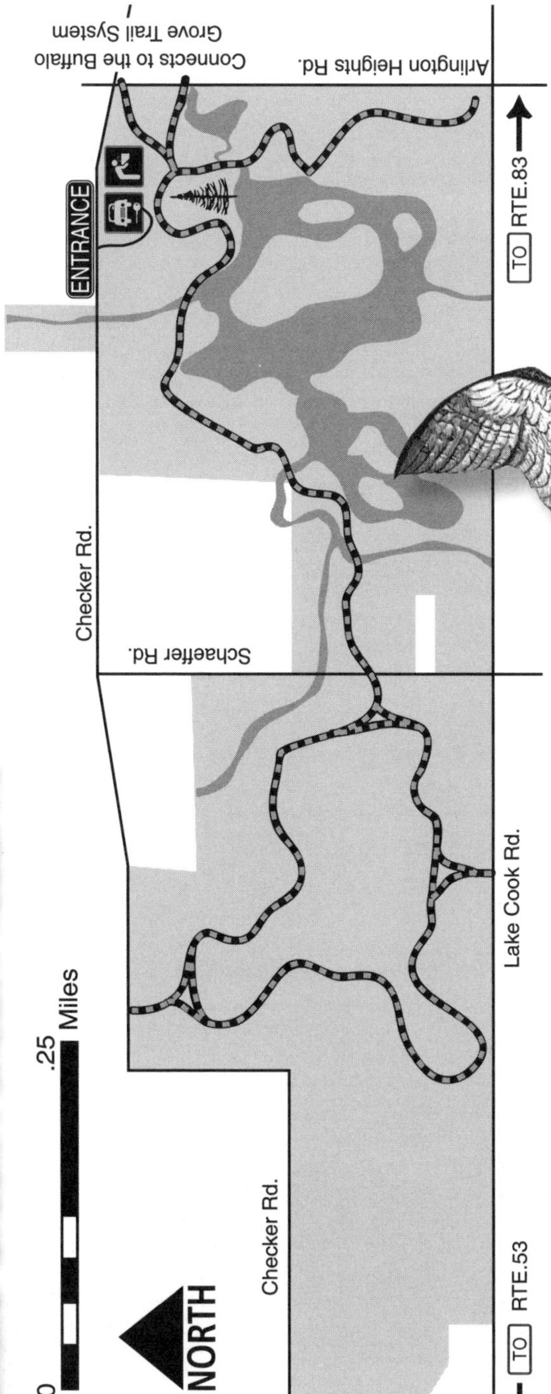

NORTH

0 .25 Miles

Checker Rd.

TO RTE.53

Lake Cook Rd.

Schaeffer Rd.

Checker Rd.

Arlington Heights Rd.

TO RTE.83

Connects to the Buffalo
Grove Trail System

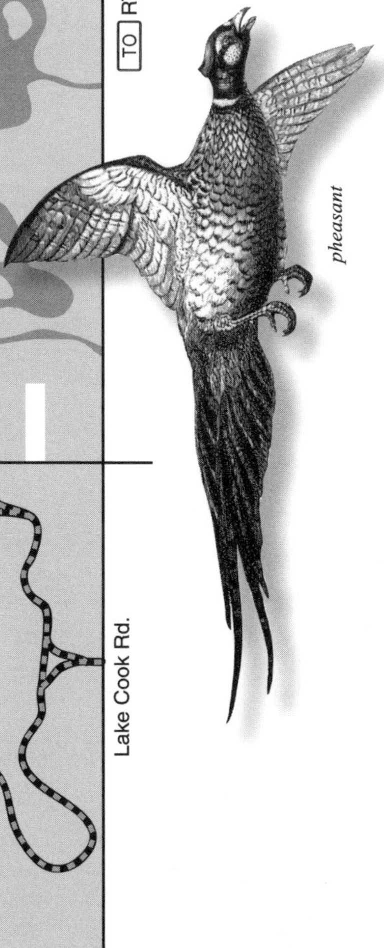

ENTRANCE

pheasant

Buffalo Grove's Trails

The Village of Buffalo Grove has taken an early lead in the development of bike, hiking and jogging paths in Lake County. Today there are over 45 miles of multi-use paths, of which 21 miles are 8 to 10 foot wide asphalt, and 24 miles of 8 to10 foot wide concrete sidewalk. Many of the paths interconnect with surrounding communities. To the west off Arlington Heights Road, a path connects to the Buffalo Creek Forest Preserve. There is also a planned connection to the Des Planes River Trail. Within the village, there are bike paths practically everywhere, to parks and schools, and along the golf courses. Residents can now bike to work, shopping, schools, churches and the parks.

rabbits

Getting there:

Major access roads into Buffalo Grove are Dundee Road to the south, Milwaukee Avenue to the east, Arlington Heights Road to the west, and Route 45 to the north. Parking near a trail access is readily available. Suggestions include Busch Grove Community Park at Deerfield Parkway and Buffalo Grove Road, the Buffalo Creek Forest Preserve off Checker Road west of Arlington Heights Road, or the Arboretum Golf Course south of Half Day Road and east of Buffalo Grove Road.

For more information:

Buffalo Grove City Hall
847-459-2500

Buffalo Grove's Trails

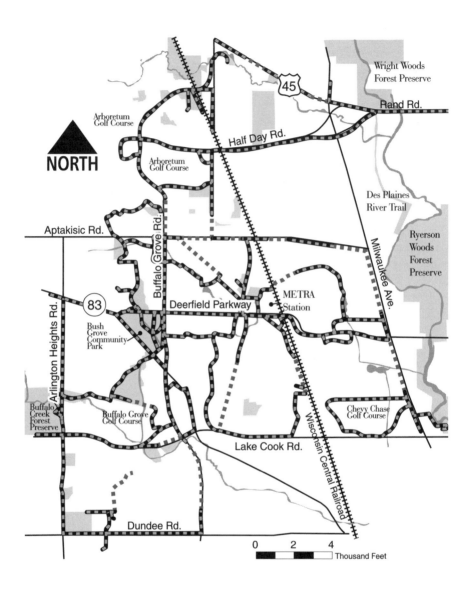

NORTH

Wright Woods Forest Preserve

Rand Rd.

Arboretum Golf Course

Half Day Rd.

Arboretum Golf Course

Des Plaines River Trail

Ryerson Woods Forest Preserve

Aptakisic Rd.

Buffalo Grove Rd.

Milwaukee Ave.

METRA Station

Deerfield Parkway

Arlington Heights Rd.

Bush Grove Community Park

Buffalo Creek Forest Preserve

Buffalo Grove Golf Course

Chevy Chase Golf Course

Wisconsin Central Railroad

Lake Cook Rd.

Dundee Rd.

0 2 4 Thousand Feet

Chain O-Lakes Bike Path

This 3 mile asphalt paved trail first opened in 2003. It parallels the south side of Rollins Road from Sayton Road eastward to where it connects to the Grant Woods Forest Preserve Trail, .8 miles east of Wilson Road. There is an underpass at Route 59, but it's a road crossing at Wilson Road.

Getting There:

Fox Lake is located in northwest Lake County. From the south take Route 59 north to Rollins Road. From the east take Belvidere Road (Route 120) to Cedar Lake Road, then north to Rollins Road.

For more information:

Lake County Division of Transportation
847-362-3750

wood duck

Chain O-Lakes Bike Path

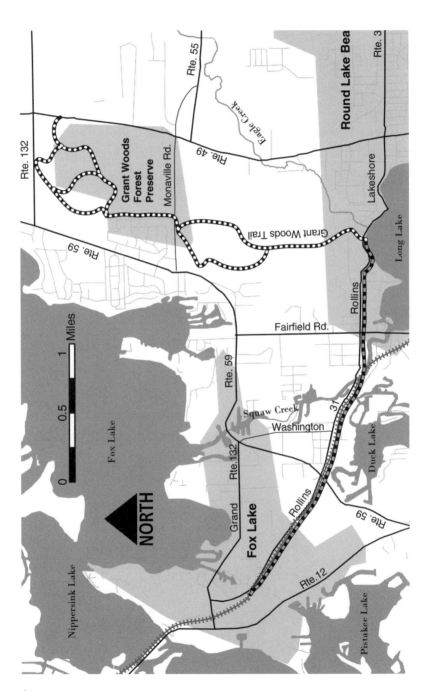

Chain O-Lakes State Park

Located in northwest Lake County, Chain O'Lakes State Park borders three natural lakes – Grass, Marie and Nippersink – and the Fox River that connects the seven other lakes that make up the chain (Bluff, Fox, Pistakee, Channel, Petite, Catherine and Redhead). The 2,793 acre state park and adjoining 3,230 acres conservation area is 60 miles northwest of Chicago, and 20 miles west of Lake Michigan.

Louis Jolliet and Jacques Marquette passed through in 1673 as they traveled the Fox River during their Illinois explorations. At that time the Chain O'Lakes area was inhabited by central Algonquin tribes, with the Miami, Mascouten and Potawatomi the predominant tribes in the region.

There are some 16 miles of hiking trails and 6 miles of biking trails. The surface is limestone screenings. These trails can be accessed at any picnic area between the park office and the concession stand. Bike rentals are available. There is also an equestrian trail with three loops with a total length of 8 miles. Horses can be rented at the park or you can bring your own.

Chain O-Lakes State Park

Chain O'Lakes State Park is open throughout the year, except Christmas. Summer hours, from May 1 through October 31, are 6 a.m. to 9 p.m. Winter hours are from 8 a.m. until sunset. From the Wilmot Road entrance, follow the park road north to its end to get to the park office. Drinking water, restrooms and bike racks are available. The office provides a great view of the valley and the Fox River, and has some interesting wildlife displays.

Each of the loop trails has a different color to identify the trail on marking posts along the pathways. The trailhead for the Gold Finch (Yellow) Trail is to the west of the park office. Turn left at the first intersection. This loop takes you along the banks of the Fox River, and through a variety of woodlands, open fields, and marshes. An occasional picnic table or bench provides an opportunity to pause and reflect.

Take a left at the next intersection to connect to the Badger (White) Trail. This area is mostly open meadow over rolling hills. Halfway through this loop there is an intersection. The path to the right takes you north back to the park office. The path to your left continues south, climbing a hill where it connects to the Sunset (Orange) Trail. Here you'll have a scenic view of the Fox River and Grass Lake in the valley below. There are several picnic areas along this path. Most areas have restrooms and drinking water.

At the next trail intersection, the path to the left takes you to the Hickory Grove picnic area and then to the Pike Marsh North picnic area. The path to the right crosses over the park road at the Deer Path picnic area and continues south through the woods. From the next intersection the path on your right takes you west to the park road, with the Red loop to the south and the Blue and Green loop to the north, across the park road past the horse trailer parking.

If you continue south on the Sunset Trail past the Pike Marsh south picnic area there is another trail intersection. The right leg takes you across the park road to the Honeysuckle Hollow campground. Beyond is Turner Lake. The path to the left proceeds south through the Oak Grove picnic area, which provides playground equipment for the kids. The Sunset Trail ends at the Maple Grove Boat Launch. Concessions, telephone, restrooms, and picnic tables are available at the Catfish Cove picnic area nearby.

From here you can either retrace your way back to the park office or continue on the Nature's Way Hiking Trail just south of the picnic area. This 2.5 mile trail passes through an oak and hickory forest, along a marsh and sedge meadow and overlooks Grass Lake. The surface is wood chips and packed earth. Expect some hills. Printed guides describing this trail are available at the park office.

Getting there:

To get to the main entrance from the north, take Route 173 to Wilmot Road and head south. From the south take Route 12 north of Fox Lake and turn north on Wilmot Road. Maps are available at the ranger station as you enter. There is also an entrance taking you to the northern area of the park off Route 173 east of Wilmot Road and west of Channel Lake. While this northern area (Oak Point) has restrooms picnic tables, shelters, and canoe/boat launch, there are no biking or hiking trails.

For more information:

Chain O'Lakes State Park
8916 Wilmot Road
Spring Grove, Illinois 60081
847-587-5512

Chain O-Lakes State Park

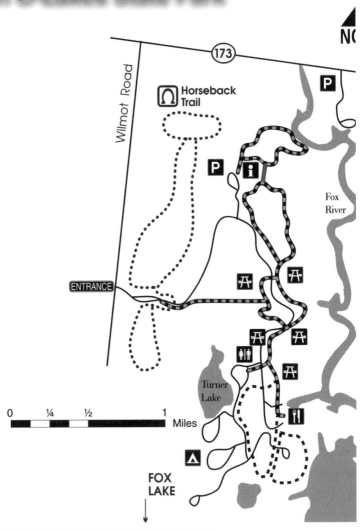

173

Wilmot Road

NO

Horseback Trail

P

Fox River

ENTRANCE

Turner Lake

0   ¼   ½   1
Miles

FOX LAKE

LEGEND

▬▬▬▬▬	Hiking/Biking Trail
▬ ▬ ▬ ▬	Hiking only Trail
▬▬▬▬▬	Alternate Trail
●●●●●●●	Horseback/Snowmobile Trail
▬ ▬ ▬ ▬	Planned Trail
┼┼┼┼┼┼┼	Railroad Tracks

Cuba Marsh Forest Preserve

Cuba Marsh offers probably the most appealing combination of marsh, woods and grassland in Lake County. Its 782 acres provide a quiet and safe opportunity to energize both mind and body.

There are two miles of crushed granite trails open to hikers, bikers and cross-country skiers. Drinking water and a restroom are available at the trailhead, which is accessible from the parking lot. The trail begins by taking you through a tall oak forest, then through a prairie with a stand of pine trees to your left. Next you pass through a marsh area, where you will cross a couple of small creeks and over some hills. The trail ends at the southeast corner of the Preserve, at Ela Road. From there you retrace your way back to the trailhead.

The setting is gently rolling hills that feature views of the marsh and scattered groves of trees. The wetland supports endangered species such as: least bitterns, pied-billed grebes and yellow-headed blackbirds. It is home to the marsh pennywort, an endangered plant. An interesting area is the dry-hill prairie on the southeast side, which is accessible during guided nature programs. It supports rare plants, such as the prairie smoke and seneca snakeroot.

Cuba Marsh Forest Preserve

Getting There:

The Preserve is located in southwestern Lake County between Barrington and Lake Zurich, west of Route 12. The entrance and parking is on the south side of Cuba Road, just west of Ela Road. The preserve is open from 6:30 a.m. to sunset.

For more information:

Lake County Forest Preserves
www.LCFPD.org
2000 North Milwaukee Ave.
Libertyville, Illinois 60048
847-367-6640

eastern bluebird

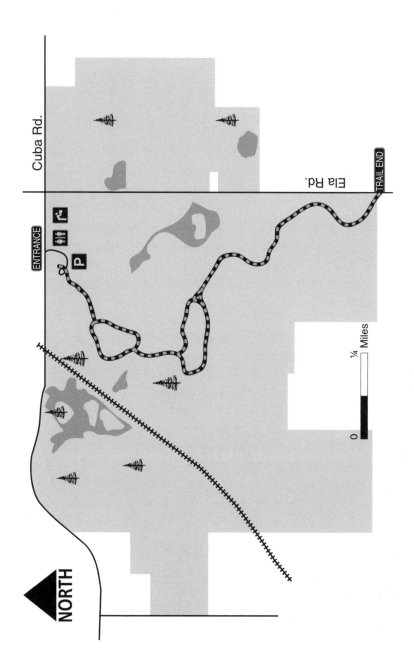

NORTH

Cuba Rd.

Ela Rd.

ENTRANCE

P

TRAIL END

0   ¼
Miles

Photo courtesy of Lake County Forest Preserves and Keith J. Portman © 2003

Des Plaines River Trail & Greenway

The Des Plaines River Greenway covers more than 7,700 acres and protects land along more than 85 percent of the river in Lake County, providing wildlife habitat, flood protection and recreation opportunities.

The multi-use, 31 mile trail connects 10 Forest Preserves and ties in over 100 miles of trails. The bridges and underpasses allow continuous travel from Wadsworth Road to Half Day Road (Route 22) without crossing any major roads. Road crossings are necessary north of Wadsworth Road and south of Half Day Road. The Des Plaines River Trail is open to hiking, biking, cross-country skiing, horseback riding, and snowmobiling (north of Independence Grove in Libertyville only). At the intersections, signs indicate which uses are allowed on the other local trails. This trail is just one leg of a whole trail network that includes the North Shore Bike Path, the McClory Trail and the Millennium Trail.

The trail provides access to a 1.2 mile asphalt paved community path along the north side of Washington Street running between Milwaukee Avenue and a little west of O'Plaine Road. The short .2 mile eastbound path that you'll see south of Washington Street and a large retention pond exits on a street providing entrance

Des Plaines River Trail & Greenway

to the Gurnee Water Works entrance. The North Shore Bike Path can be accessed at the Route 176 underpass. There is also the accessible east/west Lincolnshire Civic Center Path that runs along Route 22.

In northern Lake County, open areas such as prairies and savannas are common, the valley is wide and the river meanders. In southern Lake County, the river running through the valley is narrow and it runs a straighter course. You'll also see more woodland with oaks, hickories and maples.

In times past, the river would often block wildfires that would rage from west Lake County. Thus to the west of the river, prairies, savannas, and oaks, which can withstand fire are common, while maples, which cannot withstand fire, are found on the east bank of the river. The lowlands of the Greenway provide a natural benefit by reducing damage from heavy rains and snowmelt entering the river. It not only stores water, it cleanses it too. Located south of Wadsworth Road is the 550 acre Wetlands Research Project. This project undertakes large-scale research, wetland construction and management.

Preserves within the Des Plaines River Greenway referenced in this book:

Getting there:

As indicated on the following map, there are numerous access points and parking areas along the entire trail. You can refer to Wright Woods, Half Day, Old School, Independence Grove or Van Patten Woods Preserves described in this book for more specific directions. Open hours are 6:30 a.m. to sunset.

For more information:

Lake County Forest Preserves
www.LCFPD.org
2000 North Milwaukee Avenue
Libertyville, Illinois 60048
847-367-6640

Road Crossings – North to South

Route 173 .... road crossing, no light
Wadsworth Road .... road crossing, no light
Route 132 (Grand Avenue) .... underpass
Washington Street .... underpass
I-94 .... underpass
Route 137 .... underpass
Oak Spring Road .... road crossing, no light
Route 176 .... underpass
Old Rockland Road .... road crossing, no light
St. Mary's Road .... underpass
Old School Road .... road crossing, no light
St. Mary's Road .... underpass
Route 60 .... underpass
Route 22 .... underpass

foxes

Des Plaines River Trail & Greenway

MILE SCALE

0   1/2   1   2

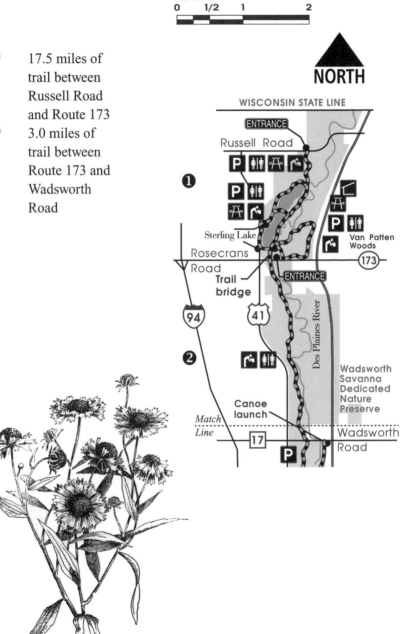

NORTH

❶ 17.5 miles of trail between Russell Road and Route 173

❷ 3.0 miles of trail between Route 173 and Wadsworth Road

WISCONSIN STATE LINE

ENTRANCE

Russell Road

❶

Sterling Lake

Rosecrans Road

Trail bridge

ENTRANCE

94

41

❷

Van Patten Woods

173

Des Plaines River

Wadsworth Savanna Dedicated Nature Preserve

Canoe launch

Match Line

17

Wadsworth Road

sneezewood

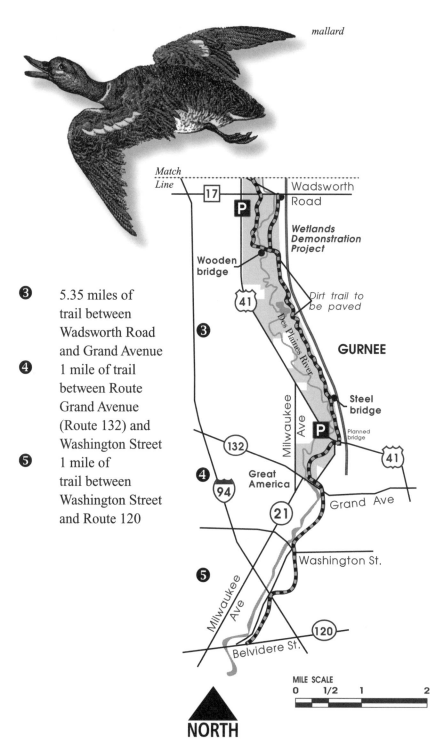

mallard

Match Line

17

P

Wadsworth Road

Wetlands Demonstration Project

Wooden bridge

41

Dirt trail to be paved

Des Plaines River

GURNEE

3 5.35 miles of trail between Wadsworth Road and Grand Avenue

4 1 mile of trail between Route Grand Avenue (Route 132) and Washington Street

5 1 mile of trail between Washington Street and Route 120

3

Milwaukee Ave

P

Steel bridge

Planned bridge

41

132

4

94

Great America

21

Grand Ave

Washington St.

5

Milwaukee Ave

120

Belvidere St.

MILE SCALE
0   1/2   1   2

NORTH

Des Plaines River Trail & Greenway

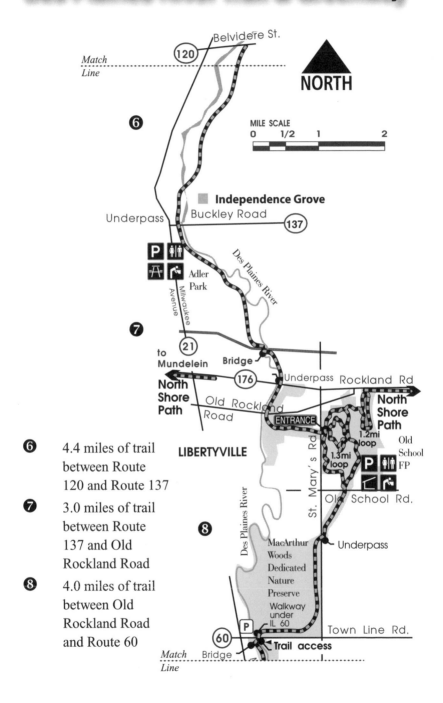

NORTH

MILE SCALE
0   1/2   1   2

Independence Grove

Buckley Road ⓻137⟩

Underpass

Des Plaines River

Adler Park

Milwaukee Avenue

to Mundelein ⟨21⟩ Bridge

North Shore Path

⟨176⟩ Underpass   Rockland Rd

Old Rockland Road

ENTRANCE

North Shore Path

LIBERTYVILLE

St. Mary's Rd

1.2mi loop

1.3mi loop

Old School FP

Old School Rd.

Des Plaines River

MacArthur Woods Dedicated Nature Preserve

Walkway under IL 60

Underpass

Town Line Rd.

⟨60⟩ Bridge **Trail access**

Match Line

Belvidere St. ⟨120⟩

Match Line

❻ 4.4 miles of trail between Route 120 and Route 137

❼ 3.0 miles of trail between Route 137 and Old Rockland Road

❽ 4.0 miles of trail between Old Rockland Road and Route 60

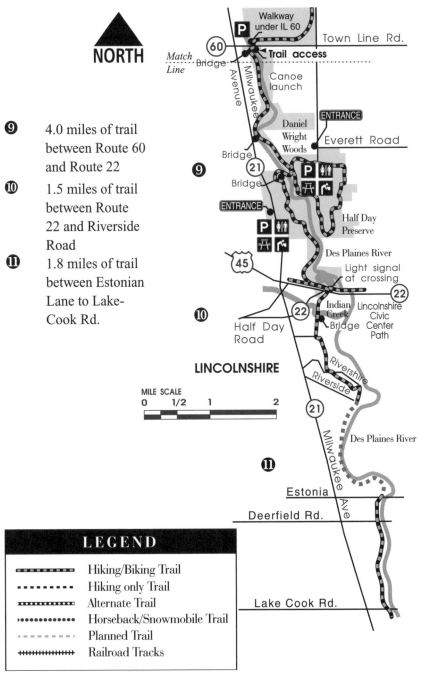

9   4.0 miles of trail between Route 60 and Route 22

10   1.5 miles of trail between Route 22 and Riverside Road

11   1.8 miles of trail between Estonian Lane to Lake-Cook Rd.

NORTH

Walkway under IL 60

Town Line Rd.

P

Match Line   Bridge

Trail access

60

Canoe launch

Milwaukee Avenue

ENTRANCE

Daniel Wright Woods

Everett Road

Bridge

9

21

Bridge

P

ENTRANCE

P

Half Day Preserve

45

Des Plaines River

Light signal at crossing

10

22

Indian Creek Bridge

22

Lincolnshire Civic Center Path

Half Day Road

LINCOLNSHIRE

Rivershire

Riverside

MILE SCALE

0   1/2   1   2

21

Des Plaines River

Milwaukee Ave

11

Estonia

Deerfield Rd.

Lake Cook Rd.

LEGEND

▪▪▪▪▪▪▪▪	Hiking/Biking Trail
▪ ▪ ▪ ▪ ▪	Hiking only Trail
▪▪▪▪▪▪▪	Alternate Trail
◆◆◆◆◆◆	Horseback/Snowmobile Trail
- - - - -	Planned Trail
+++++++	Railroad Tracks

Fox River Preserve & Marina

Situated along a peaceful stretch of the Fox River, this 517 acre Preserve is a sanctuary for people and wildlife. Its rich natural areas include rolling topography, oak savannas and high-quality wetlands that support several native species and offer habitat protection for diverse wildlife.

In some sections, the Preserve's hilly landscape is typical of southern Wisconsin's Kettle Moraine area. Unique to the site are a large rookery home to great blue herons and egrets, and a fen that supports two state-listed plant species, the downy willow herb and the northern gooseberry.

There are two miles of trail open to hiking, biking and cross-country skiing. The marina contains 169 slips. There is a four-lane launch for boats, and indoor storage is available.

Getting there:

The Fox River Preserve and Marina is located in southwest Lake County near Lake Barrington. The entrance and parking area are located on Roberts Road west of Route 59.

For more information:

Lake County Forest Preserves
www.LCFPD.org
2000 North Milwaukee Avenue
Libertyville, Illinois 60048
847-367-6640

Photo courtesy of Lake County Forest Preserves and Keith J. Portman © 2003

Fox River Preserve & Marina

Photo courtesy of Lake County Forest Preserves and Keith J. Portman © 2003

Photo courtesy of Lake County Forest Preserves and Keith J. Portman © 2003

Photo courtesy of Lake County Forest Preserves and Keith J. Portman © 2003

Grand Illinois Trail

With the growing network of trails in northern Illinois, the Illinois Dept of Transportation sponsored a "Grand Illinois Trail" in the mid 1990s' in conjunction with other state agencies, regional coalitions, local communities, conservation districts and non-profit organizations. Its 475 miles will loop between Lake Michigan and the Mississippi River as it joins together existing and proposed trails to create the state's longest continuous trail. The trail hugs historic canals, crosses unglaciated hills, parallels the Rock and Fox Rivers, and includes one of America's first rail-trails.

In Lake County, the Grand Illinois Trail incorporates the North Shore Trail and portions of the Des Plaines River Trails and Robert McClory Bike Path. There are three north-south Grand Illinois Trails corridors planned for northeastern Illinois – the Fox River, Des Plaines River, and the Chicago Lakefront/North Branch/ Green Bay/McClory Trails.

american robin

Chicago Lakefront Path: 18.5 miles; Lincoln Park to Jackson Park. Features spectacular views of Lake Michigan and the Chicago city skyline.

McClory/Green Bay/North Branch Trails: 29.5 miles plus street connections. Joins lakefront communities with wooded open space along the North Branch and Chicago River.

Des Plaines River Trail: 26 miles; from the North Shore Path to River Forest. Stretches along the forest preserves lining the Des Plaines River in Lake and Cook Counties, through wooded bottomlands and suburban communities.

North Shore Path: 8 miles; Lake Bluff to Mundelein. Crosses Lake County communities and countryside.

Chicago on-street route: 14 miles; Chicago Lakefront Path to Illinois Prairie Path. Through city neighborhoods and suburban communities.

Illinois Prairie Path: 30 miles; Maywood to Elgin. A serene green corridor through western Chicago suburbs.

Burnham Greenway: 7 miles; Chicago Lakefront Path to the Old Plank Road Trail.

Fox River Trail: 10 miles; Elgin Branch of the Illinois Prairie Path to Algonquin. Winds along the Fox River through a forest preserve, small communities, and Elgin.

Prairie Trail: 22 miles; Algonquin to Richmond. Travel across the Fox River, along native prairie, wetlands, wooded areas, and local communities.

Grand Illinois Trail

Long Prairie Trail: 14.2 miles; across the width of Boone County. A rail-trail featuring diverse prairie, rolling farm fields, woodlands and rural communities.

Rock River Recreation Path System: 10 miles, from the 1.2 mile Davis-Pecatonica Path to the Willow Creek Path. Consists of urban paths meandering along the Rock River and through parks in the Rockford area.

Willow Creek Path: 5 miles from the Rock River Recreation Path to Rock Cut State Park.

Pecatonica Prairie Path: 29 miles from the Davis-Pecatonica Path to the Jane Addams Trail. Rolling countryside with views of the Pecatonica River.

Jane Addams Trail: 13 miles between the Pecatonica Prairie Path near Freeport and Orangeville. A scenic rail-trail lined with shade trees in Stephenson County.

On-Road Routes Proposed

Across McHenry County from Richmond to Harvard, along local roads.

From the Jane Adams Trail to Galena along local roads and past the Apple River Canyon State Park and Lake Le-Aqua-Na State Park.

Southern Section's Trails

Old Plank Road Trail: 23 miles; Park Forest to Joliet. A rail-trail connecting communities in Will and southern Cook County, passing prairies and forest preserves.

I&M Canal State Trail: 55 miles; Joliet to LaSalle. Follows the old canal towpath, with views of gently rolling countryside, wooded areas, and canal communities. Passes restored aqueducts and locks.

Hennepin Canal State Trail: 79 miles; Bureau to Colona. Built on an old canal towpath, with views of canal aqueducts, restored locks, and rolling countryside.

Kaskaskia-Alliance Trail (planned): Would connect the I&M Canal State Trail and the Hennepin Canal State Trail.

Grand Illinois Trail-Carmon Cliff: Connects the Hennepin Canal State Trail and The Great River Trail through Colona and Carbon Cliff.

Western Section's Trails

Great River Trail: 53 miles (will be 65 miles when complete); Moline to Thomson, and will extend to Savanna. Take in the panoramic Mississippi River view, backwater habitats, small river communities, and the hills of Illinois' northwest corner. Some of the segments are on-road routes.

On-Road Routes (proposed): Will stretch from Savanna to Galena through the Savanna Army Depot area. For now the trail corridor will follow local roads.

For more information:

Illinois Dept. of Natural Resources
524 S. Second Street
Springfield, IL 62701
217-285-0067

Grand Illinois Trail

NORTH

Dubuque

Warren

Wisconsin

Galena

Jo Daviess

Lena

Stephenson

Jane
Addams
Trail

Winnebago

90

Freeport

Rockford

Pecatonica Prairie Path

Forreston

Ogle

Byron

Mount Carroll

Mount Morris
Oregon

Mississippi River

Carroll

Milledgeville

Polo

Iowa

Great
River
Trail

Fulton

Clinton

Di o n

88

Morrison

Sterling

Lee

Whiteside

Amboy

rie

Illinois

280

Davenport

Hennepin
Canal State Trail

Walnut

Moline

Rock Island

Geneseo

Anna a n

Bureau

Kaskaskia-
Alliance Trail

Orion

Henry

Sheffield

Princeton

Ladd

Cambridge

Depue

Ke a nee

Granville

Mercer

74

Putnam

Galva

Bradford

Henry

Stark

Ale is

Marshall

Galesburg

Lacon

Underdevelopment/Proposed

Connecting

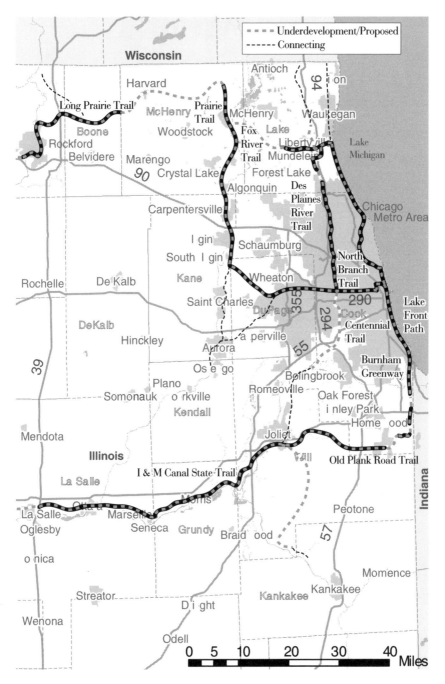

Grant Woods Forest Preserve

Grant Woods is a 1,118 acre Preserve with a gently rolling landscape of woodlands, prairie and marsh. It's located in northwestern Lake County near Lake Villa and Fox Lake.

The trail length is 6 miles and its surface is crushed granite. It can be accessed from the parking area off Monaville Road. Drinking water, restroom, picnic tables, and telephone facilities are available here. A short distance from this trailhead is an intersection. This is the beginning of a loop, so either direction will take you south around a large marsh surrounded by forest. The path in this area is wide and generally flat, along open meadow or prairie.

Continue south past the southern tip of the loop to an intersection where the trail takes off in separate directions. The trail's south leg takes you to Rollins Road about a ¼ mile distant. The eastbound leg takes you through deep woods and areas of wildflowers and ends at Fairfield road, a distance of .6 miles. There is another entrance off Grand Avenue (Route 132) at the north end of the Preserve, between Route 59 and Fairfield Road. Drinking water and restrooms facilities are available here. This section takes you through deep woods with some dips and curves. From the parking area, the trail shortly comes to a three-way intersection. All legs head south and each form sides of two joining loops. Continuing south from the western loop will connect you to the main trail south of Rollins Road. As you'll see on the map there are additional legs taking you to Route 59 and Fairfield Road.

Lake County's only known stand of wild Kentucky coffee trees grows here. These large, shiny seeds were used by the Native Americans in this area for games and for trade.

Getting there:

The main entrance is located on the south side of Monaville Road, one mile east of Route 59, and .8 miles west of Fairfield Road. The two acre Rubber Duck Pond is located near this entrance, and is stocked for fishing. The Preserve is open from 6:30 a.m. to sunset.

For more information:

Lake County Forest Preserves
www.LCFPD.org
2000 North Milwaukee Avenue
Libertyville, Illinois 60048
847-367-6640

rabbit

Grant Woods Forest Preserve

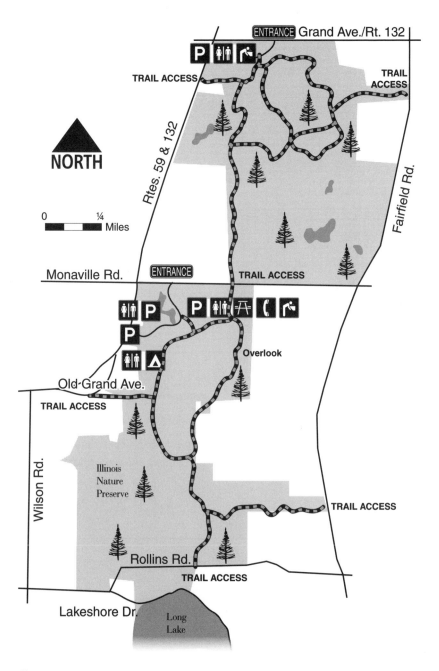

ENTRANCE Grand Ave./Rt. 132

TRAIL ACCESS

TRAIL ACCESS

NORTH

Rtes. 59 & 132

Fairfield Rd.

0   ¼
     Miles

Monaville Rd.   ENTRANCE   TRAIL ACCESS

Overlook

Old Grand Ave.

TRAIL ACCESS

Wilson Rd.

Illinois
Nature
Preserve

TRAIL ACCESS

Rollins Rd.

TRAIL ACCESS

Lakeshore Dr.   Long
                 Lake

Grassy Lake Forest Preserve

Grassy Lake is located near Lake Barrington in southwest Lake County. Its 551 acres consists of gently rolling hills, oak woodlands, marshes and moraines. Nearby is the 517 acre Fox River Preserve and Marina.

There are 3.5 miles of trails open to hiking, jogging and cross-country skiing. Bicycles are not allowed. Dogs must be on leash and picked up after. The trail winds through sedge meadows and mature oak woods, and offers scenic views of Grassy Lake and the Fox River valley. A rare natural feature is the 100 acre Wagner Fen. It provides a valuable wetland to endangered species such as the beaked spike rush and the bog violet.

Getting there:

Park at the Lake Barrington Village Hall, which is located on Old Barrington Road just west of Miller Road in Lake Barrington. The Preserve is open from 6:30 a.m. to sunset.

For more information:

Lake County Forest Preserves
www.LCFPD.org
2000 North Milwaukee Avenue
Libertyville, Illinois 60048
847 367-6640

Grassy Lake Forest Preserve

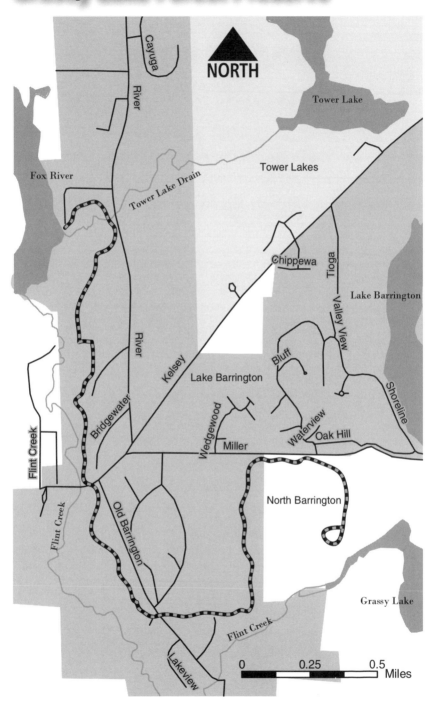

NORTH

Cayuga River

Tower Lake

Fox River

Tower Lake Drain

Tower Lakes

Chippewa

Tioga

Valley View

Lake Barrington

River

Kelsey

Lake Barrington

Bluff

Shoreline

Flint Creek

Bridgewater

Wedgewood

Waterview

Oak Hill

Miller

Flint Creek

Old Barrington

North Barrington

Flint Creek

Grassy Lake

Flint Creek

Lakeview

0   0.25   0.5
                          Miles

Greenbelt Forest Preserve

The Greenbelt Forest Preserve is nestled between the cities of Waukegan and North Chicago. Its landscape is mostly open with wetlands, prairie and oak groves. The Preserve includes a surprising array of birds and wildflowers within its 558 acres.

There are two trails open for hiking, bicycling and cross-country skiing. Total length is 5 miles of which 4 miles are open to biking and cross-country skiing. The topography is mostly flat and the surface is crushed granite for easy travel. There is parking with trail access in the western section by continuing either west or north from the entrance road junction. Take the north leg for drinking water, restroom, shelters and picnic facilities. The 1 mile loop around a marsh includes a series of signs that tell about the area. It connects to a .75 mile loop that goes around Pulaski Lake.

You can also access the eastern section by taking Green Bay Road south .5 miles south of Belvidere Road (Route 120) to 10th Street, then east for .7 miles and turn right on Dugdale Road. The entrance is .2 miles on the right. There is a .75 mile loop around Dugdale Lake, which connects to a 1.5 mile loop through open landscape. Here you'll also find multiple fitness stations, drinking water and restrooms.

Greenbelt Forest Preserve

The new multi-purpose Greenbelt Cultural Center in the eastern section provides a fantastic setting for educational and cultural programs. The Center holds up to 250 people, and can be rented for meetings, weddings, and other events.

Greenbelt sits atop the mid-continental divide. That means any rain falling on the east side of Green Bay Road heads for the Atlantic Ocean, while any falling on the west side heads for the Gulf of Mexico.

Getting There:

You can get to both the western and eastern sections by taking Green Bay Road south of Belvidere Road for .7 miles. The entrance to the western section is on the right, and the eastern section, with Visitors Center, is on the left. You can also get to the eastern section by taking Green Bay Road south .5 miles south of Belvidere Road (Route 120) to 10th Street, then east for .7 miles and turn right on Dugdale Road. There is an entrance .2 miles on the right. The Preserve is open from 6:30 a.m. to sunset.

For more information:

Lake County Forest Preserves
www.LCFPD.org
2000 North Milwaukee Avenue
Libertyville, Illinois 60048
847-367-6640

hawk

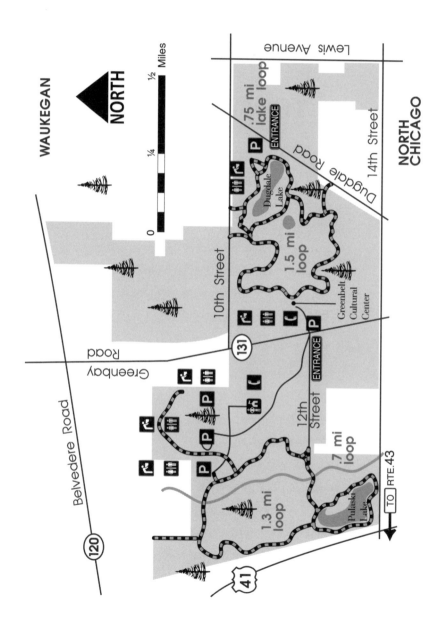

WAUKEGAN

NORTH

¼   ½ Miles

0

Lewis Avenue

NORTH CHICAGO

.75 mi lake loop

ENTRANCE

Dugdale Lake

1.5 mi loop

Dugdale Road

14th Street

10th Street

Greenbay Road

131

Greenbelt Cultural Center

ENTRANCE

12th Street

.7 mi loop

Belvedere Road

120

1.3 mi loop

Pulaski Lake

41

TO RTE. 43

Half Day & Wright Woods Forest Preserves

These two Forest Preserves are adjacent to each other near Vernon Hills and Lincolnshire in southeastern Lake County. Half Day consists of 201 acres, while Wright Woods has 327 acres. The Des Plaines River Trail passes through these two preserves. Wright Woods has an additional four miles of looped trails open to hikers, bicyclists and cross-country skiers. Half Day has several short trails branching off the parking areas and connecting to the Des Plaines River Trail. Trail surfaces are crushed granite.

The Des Plaines River frequently stopped the wildfires that often swept across Lake County prior to settlement by Europeans. As a result, Half Day supports oaks and prairie plants that thrived under fire's influence. Wright Woods, on the other hand, supports large stands of maples, which are less tolerant of fire. These maples make it a great place to enjoy the autumn colors. Contrary to the popular belief that Half Day was the time it took to travel from Chicago, it was really named after Chief Half Day of the Potowatomi Indians. Wright Woods is named for Captain Daniel Wright, one of Lake County's early settlers. Both preserves offer drinking water, restrooms and playgrounds. Half Day also offers picnic shelters. There is a large grass field at Half Day that can be used for volleyball, kite flying and other activities.

Getting There:

The Half Day entrance is located on Milwaukee Avenue (Route 21), 2 miles south of Route 60 near Vernon Hills. The Wright Woods entrance is at St. Mary's and Everett Roads, 1.5 miles south of Route 60 and is near Lincolnshire. Open hours are from 6:30 a.m. to sunset.

For more information:

Lake County Forest Preserves
www.LCFPD.org
2000 North Milwaukee Avenue
Libertyville, Illinois 60048
(847) 367-6640

sparrow hawk

Half Day & Wright Woods Forest Preserves

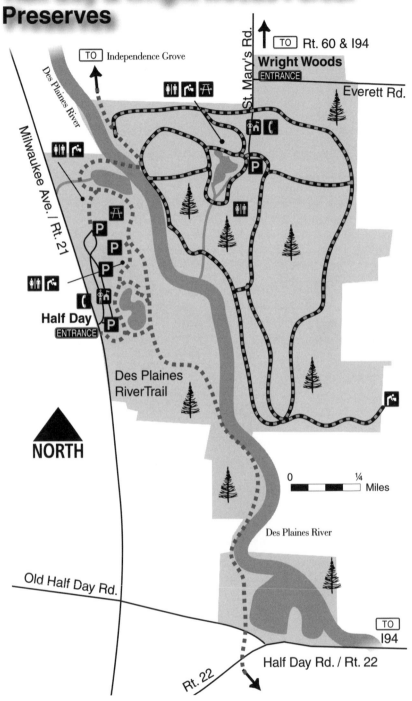

TO Independence Grove

Des Plaines River

St. Mary's Rd.

TO Rt. 60 & I94

Wright Woods
ENTRANCE

Everett Rd.

Milwaukee Ave. / Rt. 21

Half Day
ENTRANCE

Des Plaines RiverTrail

NORTH

0   ¼
Miles

Des Plaines River

Old Half Day Rd.

TO I94

Rt. 22

Half Day Rd. / Rt. 22

Illinois Beach State Park

Stretching for 6 ½ miles along the sandy shore of Lake Michigan in the northeast corner of Illinois, Illinois Beach State Park encompasses the only remaining beach ridge shoreline in the state. This 4,160 acre park, consisting of two separate areas, offers opportunities for hiking, bicycling, camping, picnicking, walking its sandy beaches, and swimming the chilly waters of Lake Michigan.

There are some 12 miles of trails, of which approximately 8 miles are open to biking. The surface is a mixture of crushed gravel, woodchip and sand.

The park has dramatic ridges and swales, sprawling marshes, dunes, forest of oak and a array of animal and plant species. Large expanses of marsh in the swales support dense stands of cattail, bluepoint grass, reed grass, big bluestem, prairie cordgrass and sedges. Black oak trees, open and savanna-like, top the sandy ridges. Just north of a stand of pines in the southern area is the Dead River that is blocked by a sand bar much of the year, forming a pond. When the water rises sufficiently, it breaks through the sandbar and drains the surrounding marshes.

Illinois Beach State Park

The Visitor Center is open daily during the summer and on weekends in spring and fall. An interpreter is on duty to answer your questions. Picnic sites are provided throughout the park and camping is available in the south unit. Lodging is available at the Illinois Beach Resort and Conference Center in the southern unit. The North Point Marina, with 1,500 slips, is accessible from 7th Street in the northern unit.

Getting there:

South Unit

The main entrance is on Wadsworth Road, east off Sheridan Road (Route 173), north of Waukegan and just south of Zion. Follow the signs to the nature preserve, about 1.2 miles past the railroad tracks.

North Unit

There are two access roads to parking and the trails. In Zion, take 17th Street east off Sheridan to parking at Sand Pond or in the Dunes Day Use Area at the end of the road.

The other entrance is off 7th Street east of Sheridan Road in Winthrop Harbor. Turn right at the Harbor Administration Building. The next right takes you to the parking area and a gravel road leading to the trail.

For more information:

Illinois Beach State Park
Zion, Illinois 60099
847-662-4811

common gull

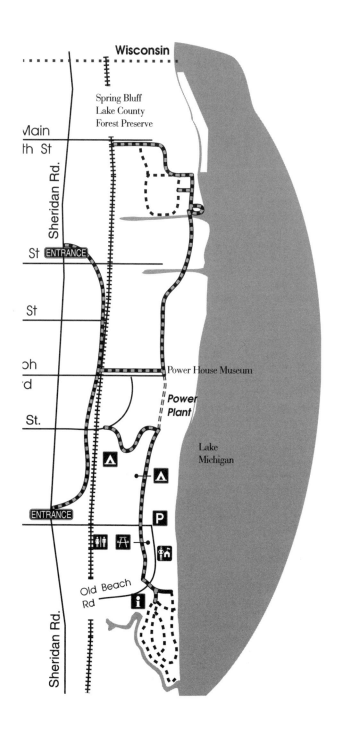

Wisconsin

Spring Bluff
Lake County
Forest Preserve

Main

th St

Sheridan Rd.

St ENTRANCE

St

oh

d

St.

Power House Museum

**Power
Plant**

Lake
Michigan

ENTRANCE

Old Beach
Rd

Sheridan Rd.

Independence Grove Forest Preserve

Independence Grove is located in central Lake County near Libertyville and is set in the broad valley of the Des Plaines River.

The Preserve provides a wide range of outdoor and education opportunities centered on a 115 acre lake reclaimed from an old gravel quarry. Parking is free for Lake County residents, but there is an entrance fee for non-residents.

There are nearly 7 miles of trail that wind throughout the Preserve. The 2.3 mile Lakeside Trail meanders around the lake. The surface is crushed granite and is ideal for hiking, biking and jogging. The 2.5 mile Overlook Trail is paved and runs through scenic areas of the Preserve. It's designed for in-line skating and general use. In addition there are two shorter trails connecting the Lakeside and Overlook Trails. The .70 mile South Bay Loop is paved, while the .75 mile North Bay Loop has a combination of asphalt and granite sections.

Independence Grove connects to the 31 mile Des Plaines River Trail as it winds through the Preserve. You can take the Des Plaines River Trail 16.4 miles north to Wisconsin or 12.5 miles south to Lincolnshire. Another 1.8 mile section is open south of Lincolnshire from Estonian Lane to Lake Cook Road near Deerfield. From there you can continue south on the Forest Preserve District of Cook County's Des Plaines Division Trail.

Facilities within Independence Grove include drinking water, restrooms, the North Bay Pavilion picnic shelter, open picnic areas, sand volleyball courts, the Leopold Point observation area, fishing, swimming beach, showers, and marina with boat rentals. The 19,000-square foot Visitors Center is located along the east shore of the lake and features a gift shop, interactive exhibits, food services and a classroom. From it spacious windows you have a panoramic view of the lake. The Center can be rented for special events. The Visitors Center and Nature Store are open from 9 a.m. to 4:30 p.m., except for holidays and special events. The nearby Millennia Plaza, with its surrounding amphitheater, fountain and native garden, makes an ideal setting for outdoor celebrations and educational programs.

Muskrats, beaver, mink, raccoon, possum and deer are some of the animals that inhabit the area. Migrating waterfowl such as greater scaup, golden eye, widgeons, mergansers, loons and red-headed ducks visit the lake each fall on their way south.

Getting there:

The entrance and parking area are located off Buckley Road (Route 137) just east of Milwaukee Avenue (Route 21) and west of River Road. Preserve hours are 6:30 a.m. to sunset.

For more information:

Lake County Forest Preserves
www.LCFPD.org
2000 North Milwaukee Avenue
Libertyville, IL 60048
847-367-6640

Independence Grove Forest Preserve

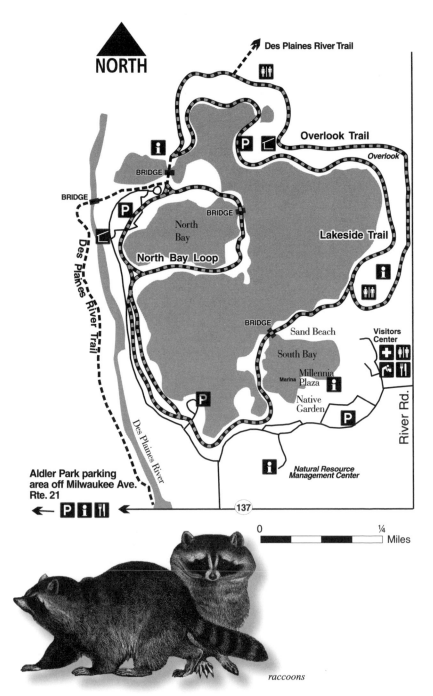

NORTH

Des Plaines River Trail

Overlook Trail

Overlook

BRIDGE

BRIDGE

North Bay

BRIDGE

North Bay Loop

Lakeside Trail

Des Plaines River Trail

BRIDGE

Sand Beach

Visitors Center

South Bay

Marina

Millennia Plaza

Native Garden

Des Plaines River

Aldler Park parking area off Milwaukee Ave. Rte. 21

Natural Resource Management Center

137

River Rd.

0   ¼ Miles

raccoons

Independence Grove Forest Preserve

Photo courtesy of Lake County Forest Preserves and Keith J. Portman © 2003

Photo courtesy of Lake County Forest Preserves and Keith J. Portman © 2003

Lake Forest's Preserves

The Lake Forest Open Lands Association is a non-profit organization for the acquisition, habitat restoration, public education, and conservation of open lands in the community. It currently maintains over 12 miles of walking trails in its six preserves.

Derwen Mawr

This 26 acre preserve contains several remnant pockets of original prairie and wetlands. It connects to and is part of the Skokie River Nature Preserve. Parking is available at the Deerpath Middle School. To get to the trails cross Deerpath at the intersection with Golf Lane, and go past the gated trailhead and kiosk.

Everett Farm

This 35 acre preserve was a former tree nursery. There are unusual trees scattered throughout the area, such catalpa, sycamore, and a grove of 80 year old pine and spruce. The eastern third of the site is a high quality woodland and wet prairie.

Access and parking are located on James Court, east off Telegraph Road, about a ½ mile north of Route 22. Park in the small lot on the north side of James Court and walk east to the trailhead and kiosk.

Lake Forest's Preserves

Mellody Farm

This 50 acre site was formerly part of the J. Ogden Armour estate, and had been heavily farmed. Since then much of the wetlands, prairies, a large oak savanna and 2,000 feet of the frontage along the Middlefork River of this preserve have been restored. During the spring and summer you'll find blooming wildflowers such as shooting start, swamp milkweed, nodding wild onion and trillium. Great egrets, blue herons and wood ducks inhabit its wetlands. The gatehouse complex has also been restored and renamed the Lockhart Family Nature Center. It now serves as Open Lands' environmental education center.

Mellody Farm Nature Preserve is located on the southwest corner of Deerpath and Waukegan Road.

Middlefork Farm

Middlefork was formerly a working farm. This 120 acre site has been largely restored. You will enjoy the sweeping views of the Middlefork Valley while among the 200-year-old bur oaks and shagbark hickories that dot the savanna.

There are several entrances on the south side of Middlefork Drive and the north side of Acorn Drive. You can park at the west end of Middlefork Drive next to the Elawa Farm buildings and walk east along the drive to the first trail entrance.

Skokie River

The 120 acre preserve consists of woodlands, savanna, sedge meadows, and a large area of rare virgin prairie. The Skokie River Nature Preserve has a north and south unit and two access points.

The northern unit access is at the west end of Laurel Avenue, west of Green Bay Road. Park at the end of Laurel and walk on the bike path across the bridge to the wood-chipped trail on the right. The southern unit access is on Deerpath, across the street from the Deerpath Middle School, just east of Golf Lane. You can park at the Deerpath Middle School.

West Skokie

This 30 acre preserve, commonly known as Mellvaine Meadow, has been completely restored to prairie and wetland. Native grasses and flowers have rebounded. The Chicago River forms the western boundary of the preserve.

Trail access and parking are located on the south side of Westleigh road, a quarter mile east of Waukegan Road.

For more information

Lake Forest Open Lands Association
272 East Deerpath, Suite 318
Lake Forest, Illinois 60045
847-234-3880

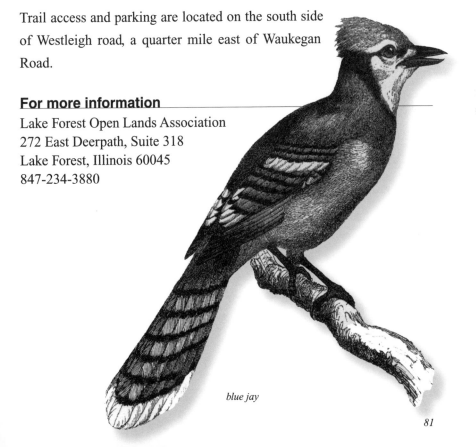

blue jay

Lake Forest's Preserves

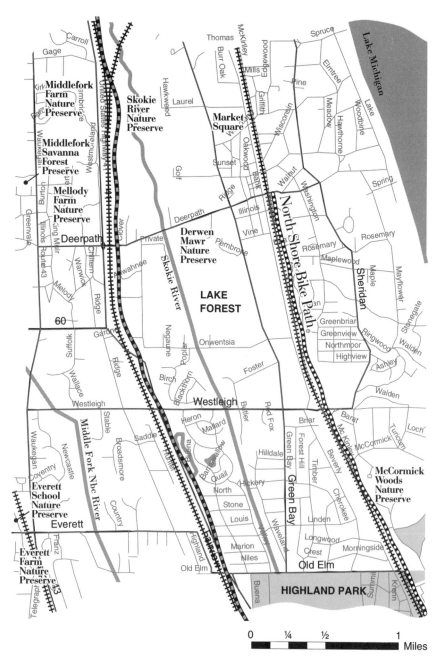

0   ¼   ½   1
Miles

Lakewood Forest Preserve and the Lake County Discovery Museum

Lakewood Forest Preserve is located near Wauconda, west of Mundelein and north of Lake Zurich, in southwestern Lake County. It is the county's largest preserve with 2,578 acres of rolling hills, dense oak woods, wetlands, fields, and several lakes and ponds. It is also home to the Lake County Discovery Museum and the Lakewood dog exercise area.

Hikers have 9 miles of looped trails that wind their way around the lakes and ponds and through the forest, and include 6.5 miles of horse trails. The trails are mostly crushed granite, wide, and generally flat. There is access to the hiking trail just off the Route 176 entrance and to the right. If you plan to hike the horse trail, take Ivanhoe Road inside the preserve to the gravel road with a sign identifying hiking and horse trails. Bicycles are not allowed on these trails.

Lakewood Forest Preserve and the Lake County Discovery Museum

The first three miles of the Millennium Trail opened in 2002. The surface is crushed granite, and is open to hiking, biking, cross-country skiing and horseback riding. It runs from the parking area off Fairfield Road, south of Route 176, through dense woodland and rolling hills. You'll find some of these hills challenging. Lakewood will eventually connect to other Forest Preserves through this planned 35 mile trail.

Activities at Lakewood include family activity days, Scout badge programs, field trips, the Farm Heritage Festival and Civil War Days. There are also summer day camps and other informative programs about history and nature, including Native Americans, and life of the early settlers. You can reserve the rustic and private tent campground for organized youth groups. A water pump, fire rings, outhouse, and firewood (when available) are provided. Permit required.

The all-new Lake County Discovery Museum is one of the ten most popular destination spots in Lake County. The Museum provides the well-rounded museum experience you expect from a big-city museum…without the traffic hassles!

Hands-on interactive exhibits introduce the history of Lake County in a fun learning environment. The Museum also displays the nation's largest permanent exhibition on the history and significance of postcards. Changing exhibits in the special exhibition gallery are designed to delight visitors of all ages and interests. A local artist gallery displays works of art from talented Chicagoland artists. The variety of programs and events offered for adults, families and school groups educate and entertain. Admission fees apply. Call 847-968-3400 for gallery hours.

Drinking water, restrooms, and electricity are available at all the shelters. Permits are needed to reserve a shelter.

Getting there:

The main entrance is on Route 176, just west of Fairfield Road. This entrance takes you to the Museum and Shelters C, D, and E. Another entrance is at the intersection of Ivanhoe and Fairfield Roads. From here go east for the Winter Sports Area; west for Shelters A and B, and horse trail parking; and north for the Dog Exercise Area. The preserve is open from 6:30 a.m. to sunset.

For more information:

Lake County Forest Preserves
www.LCFPD.org
2000 North Milwaukee Avenue
Libertyville, Illinois 60048
847-367-6640

bat

LEGEND	
▬▬▬▬▬▬	Hiking/Biking Trail
- - - - - - - -	Hiking only Trail
▭▭▭▭▭▭	Alternate Trail
●●●●●●●●●●●	Horseback/Snowmobile Trail
⸱ ⸱ ⸱ ⸱ ⸱ ⸱ ⸱ ⸱	Planned Trail
┼┼┼┼┼┼┼┼┼┼	Railroad Tracks

Lakewood Forest Preserve and the Lake County Discovery Museum

Fairfield Rd.

0 ¼ Miles

NORTH

Broberg Marsh

ENTRANCE

Dog Exercise Area

TO
Wauconda
Rte. 59
Rte. 12

Rte. 176

Banana Lake

P

P

P

P

P

P

ENTRANCE

Winter Sports Area & Mellenium Trail
(see next page)

Taylor Lake

Ivanhoe Rd.

P

Heron Pond

Fairfield Rd.

Acorn Lake

Beaver Lake

ENTRANCE

Brown Rd.

P

Rte. 12

Milton Rd.

Dragon's Lair

🏛 = Lake County Discovery Museum

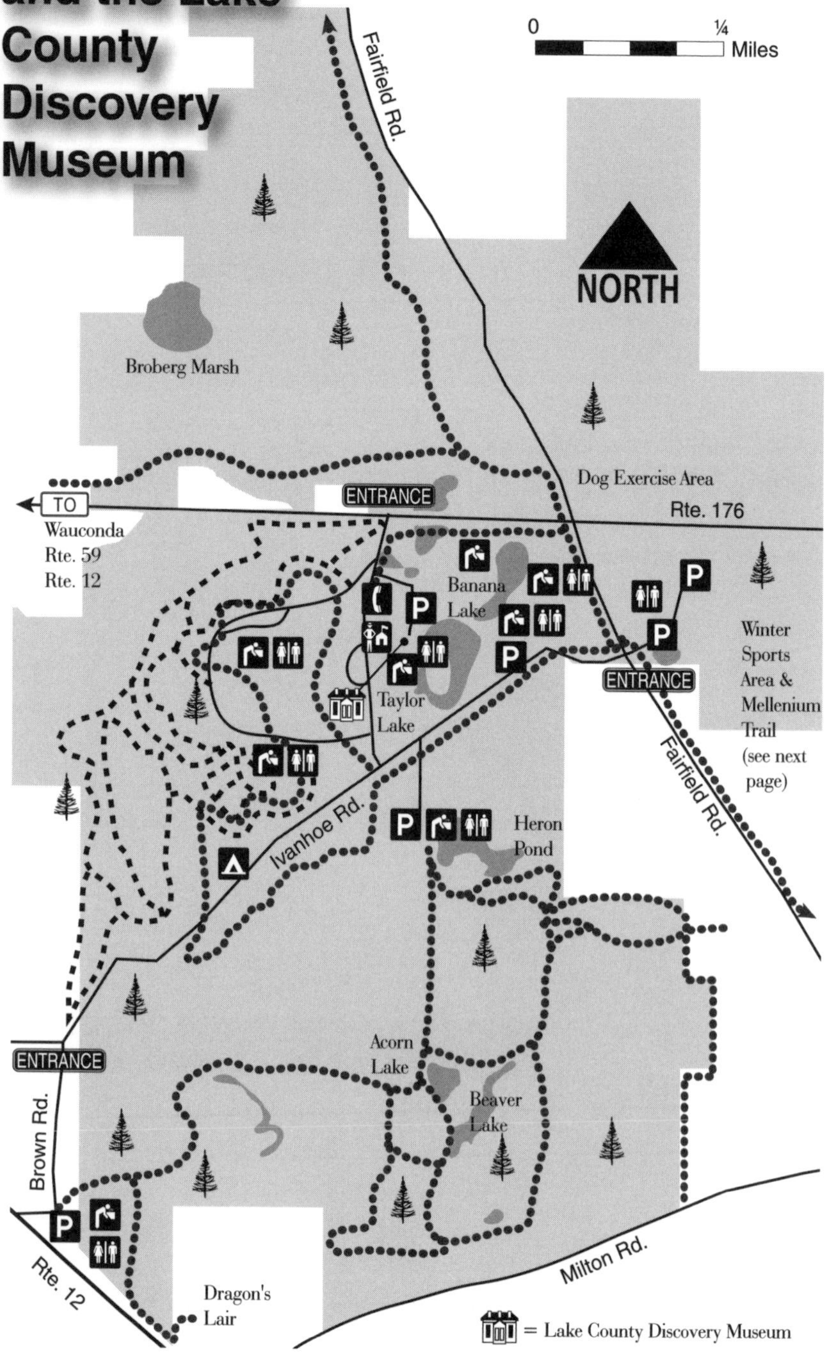

Lakewood Forest Preserve
Millenium Trail

Millenium Trail

Pond

David Lake

Pond

Pond

NORTH

Hawley Rd.

Fairfield Rd.

Lakewood Forest Preserve

Libertyville's Butler Lake Trail

This is a 3 mile, 4-6 foot wide asphalt paved path in north central Libertyville. The trail lacks a formal name, but plans call for it to encircle Butler Lake. Parking near the trail is available by the Butler Lake Park playground off Winchester Road. One route is to take the trail south, across Lake Street and around the east side of Butler Lake to the high school, where it ends. The west side of Butler Lake is currently undeveloped. There is a short eastbound leg of the trail paralleling the south side of Winchester Road and the railroad tracks. On the north side of Winchester Road a longer leg parallels the north side of these tracks. This leg in turn branches off north to Gilbert Stiles Park, and northwest to Paul M. Neal Park. The terrain is mostly flat with open areas and short stretches of woods.

Libertyville also hosts a segment of the Des Plaines River Trail to the east, and the North Shore Path as it passes along the south side of Route 176. You can access the Des Plaines River Trail by way of a path passing through Adler Park. The park entrance on Park View Drive, off Milwaukee Avenue and the first stoplight south of Route 137.

Getting there:

From Milwaukee Avenue, turn west on Winchester Road for about a mile, just past the railroad tracks to the Butler Lake Park entrance on the south side of the road. Here you'll find parking and the playgrounds.

For more information:

Libertyville Parks & Recreation Dept.
847-918-2074

Libertyville's Butler Lake Trail

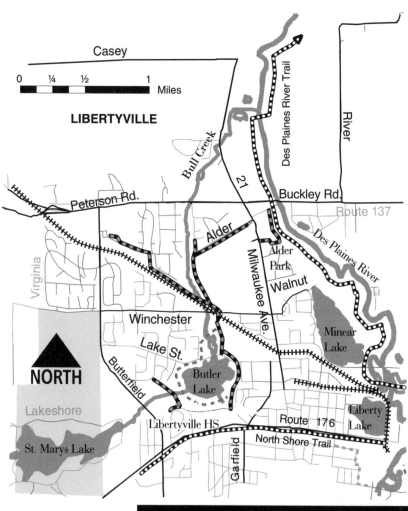

Casey

0   ¼   ½   1
Miles

LIBERTYVILLE

Bull Creek

Des Plaines River Trail

River

21

Peterson Rd.

Buckley Rd.

Route 137

Alder

Des Plaines River

Virginia

Alder Park

Walnut

Milwaukee Ave.

Winchester

Minear Lake

Lake St.

Butterfield

NORTH

Butler Lake

Lakeshore

Libertyville HS

Liberty Lake

Route 176

St. Marys Lake

North Shore Trail

Garfield

LEGEND

▪▪▪▪▪▪▪▪▪▪	Hiking/Biking Trail
▪ ▪ ▪ ▪ ▪ ▪	Hiking only Trail
✕✕✕✕✕✕✕✕	Alternate Trail
●●●●●●●●●●	Horseback/Snowmobile Trail
▪ ▪ ▪ ▪ ▪	Planned Trail
┼┼┼┼┼┼┼┼┼┼	Railroad Tracks

Lyons Woods Forest Preserve

This 264 acre Preserve offers a diverse mix of prairie, savanna, pine grove, forest and fen. The woods support large stands of white bur and black oak. Plants such as goldenrod, dropseed and big bluestem are found in the prairie.

There are 3 miles of crushed granite trails open to hikers, bicyclists and cross-country skiers. The first intersection is the southern end of a loop through a meadow. This loop in turn connects to the trail's second loop, which crosses North Avenue twice. There is access to the Robert McClory Bike Path off the trail's northwest leg. There are trail accesses but no parking at Hendee Avenue, at the North Avenue crossings, or on Blanchard Road west of North Avenue. A water pump and restrooms are located near the parking lot.

Many warblers nest here, including the yellowthroat, the ovenbird and the blue-winged warbler. The evergreens you find here were once a tree nursery, as they are not native to this area.

fox

Lyons Woods Forest Preserve

Getting there:

Lyons Woods is near Waukegan and Beach Park in northeastern Lake County. From downtown Waukegan, take Sheridan Road north to Blanchard Road and turn left. The entrance is a short distance on the right. The trailhead is located at the end of the parking area. The preserve is open from 6:30 a.m. to sunset.

For more information:

Lake County Forest Preserves
www.LCFPD.com
2000 North Milwaukee Avenue
Libertyville, Illinois 60048
(847) 367-6640

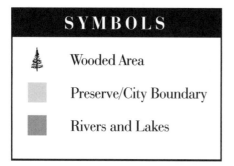

SYMBOLS

🌲 Wooded Area

Preserve/City Boundary

Rivers and Lakes

Facilities

▲ Camping
✚ First Aid
🍴 Food/Concession
ℹ Information
🛏 Lodging
P Parking
⛱ Picnic Area
🚹 Rangers Station
🚻 Restroom
🏠 Shelter
☎ Telephone
💧 Water

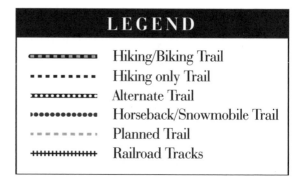

LEGEND

▬▬▬▬▬ Hiking/Biking Trail
- - - - - Hiking only Trail
✕✕✕✕✕ Alternate Trail
●●●●●● Horseback/Snowmobile Trail
- - - - - Planned Trail
╫╫╫╫╫╫ Railroad Tracks

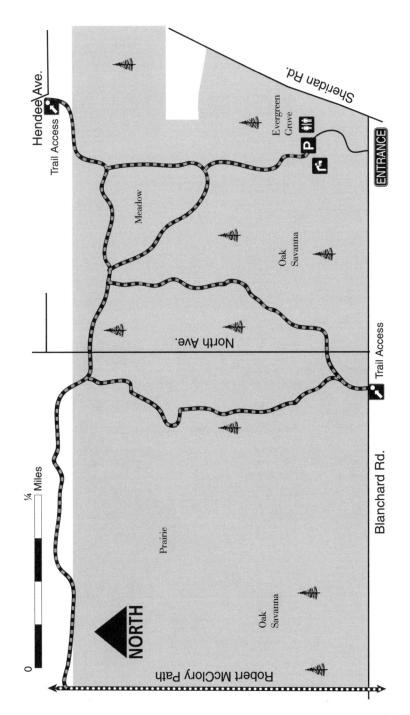

Hendee Ave.

Trail Access

Sheridan Rd.

Evergreen Grove

ENTRANCE

Meadow

Oak Savanna

North Ave.

Trail Access

Blanchard Rd.

Prairie

Oak Savanna

NORTH

Robert McClory Path

0 ¼ Miles

McDonald Woods Forest Preserve

McDonald Woods is a glacial landscape of rolling hills, steep ravines and wetlands, and a great place to hike or ride your bike! You can wander through evergreen forests and meadows nestled in a valley of solitude.

There are 4.5 miles of trail for hiking and cross-country skiing, of which 3.5 miles is crushed granite and 1 mile is wood chip. The granite trail is also open to bikers and loops around two large marsh ponds in a valley.

The steep ravines are teeming with lush vegetation including basswoods and sugar maples, seldom found growing wild in this area. McDonald Woods also features wetlands that are a haven for waterfowl, a thick pine grove, and restored prairies and oak woodlands.

pintails

Getting there:

Take Route 45 north to Grass Lake Road, then west for .7 miles to the entrance on the south side of the road. Observe the historic homes in the small town of Milburn as you approach and turn onto Grass Lake Road. The preserve is open from 6:30 to sunset.

For more information:

Lake County Forest Preserves
www.LCFPD.org
2000 North Milwaukee Avenue
Libertyville, Illinois 60048
847-367-6640

Photo courtesy of Lake County Forest Preserves and Keith J. Portman © 2003

McDonald Woods Forest Preserve

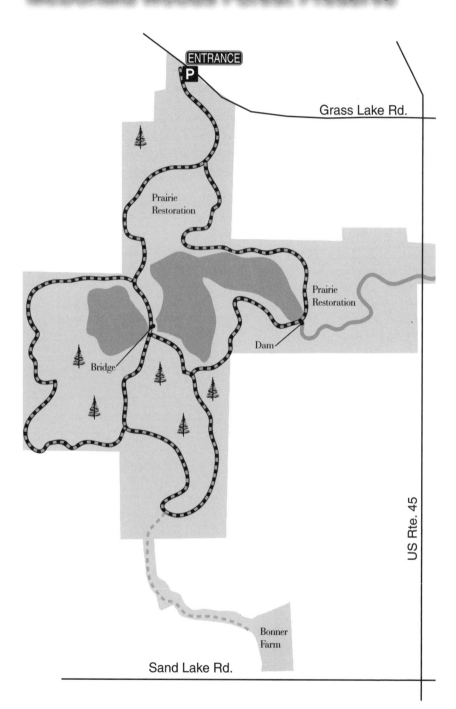

Middlefork Savanna Forest Preserve

This 567 acre Preserve is located in southeast Lake County near Lake Forest.

There are 4 miles of gravel trails open to hiking, bicycling, and cross-country skiing, plus another half mile of mowed path for hikers. Middlefork is home to a rare tallgrass savanna, and features a mix of oak savanna and woodlands, wet and mesic prairies, meadows and marshes. There are two boardwalks on the trails to help protect sensitive wetlands areas.

Middlefork supports an impressive list of uncommon birds, butterflies and other species that require large open areas for survival, and is one of the most important sites for biodiversity in northeastern Illinois. The Preserve also serves as a national ecological research site and outdoor classroom for schools and other organizations.

How to get there:

The entrance is located at Waukegan Road (Route 43) and Middlefork Drive north of Route 60 and south of Route 176. Turn west onto Middlefork Drive and follow signs to the Preserve parking area. Open hours are 6:30 a.m. to sunset.

Middlefork Savanna Forest Preserve

For more information:

Lake County Forest Preserves
www.LCFPD.org
2000 North Milwaukee Avenue
Libertyville, Illinois 60048
847-367-6640

Photo courtesy of Lake County Forest Preserves and Keith J. Portman © 2003

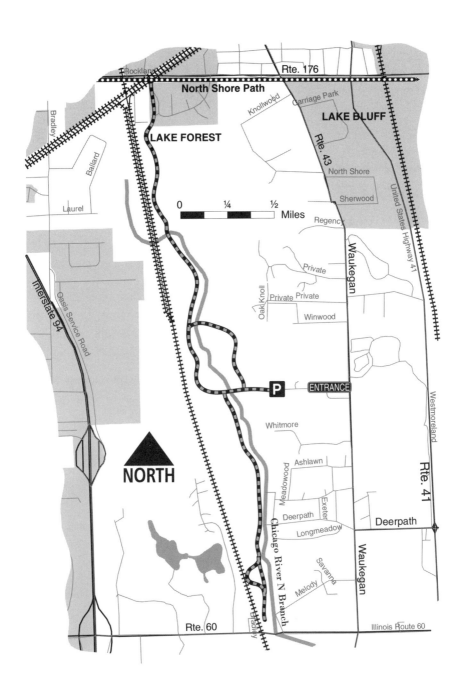

Rte. 176

North Shore Path

Rockland

Knollwood

Carriage Park

LAKE BLUFF

LAKE FOREST

Bradley

Ballard

North Shore

Rte. 43

United States Highway 41

Laurel

Sherwood

0   ¼   ½   Miles

Regency

Interstate 94

Oasis Service Road

Private

Oak Knoll

Private Private

Winwood

Waukegan

P ENTRANCE

Westmoreland

Rte. 41

Whitmore

NORTH

Ashlawn

Meadowood

Exeter

Deerpath

Deerpath

Longmeadow

Chicago River N Branch

Savanna

Melody

Waukegan

Rte. 60

Bradley

Illinois Route 60

Millennium Trail

The first 3.2 mile section of the planned 35 mile Millennium Trail to connect central, western and northern Lake County communities and Forest Preserves opened in 2002 near Wauconda.

The surface is crushed granite, and is open to hiking, biking, cross-country skiing and horseback riding. It runs from the parking area off Fairfield Road, south of Route 176 through dense woodland and rolling hills. You'll find some of these hills challenging. See page 87 for the trail map. This segment connects to the west section of the North Shore Bike Path, an asphalt paved path running along the south side of Hawley Road to Midlothian Road in Mundelein, where it currently ends.

A 7 mile section from Lakewood Forest Preserve north to Singing Hills Forest Preserve near Volo is under construction as of the publication of this book. From there plans call for the route to curve north and east from Singing Hills, to and through the Round Lake area communities to Rollins Savanna Forest Preserve near Grayslake. Then it will head north through Fourth Lake Forest Preserve. A separate, short link of the Millennium

Trail is already in place connecting Bonner Heritage Farm to McDonald Woods near Lindenhurst. Finally it will run east from there to connect with the northern sections of the Des Plaines River Trail near Wadsworth.

Getting there:

The Millennium Trail Lake Section parking area is located off Fairfield Road just south of Route 176 in the Lakewood Forest Preserve Winter Sports Area. There is a comfort station available here. The Preserve is open from 6:30 a.m. to sunset.

For more information:

Lake County Forest Preserves
www.LCFPD.org
2000 North Milwaukee Ave.
Libertyville, Illinois 60048
847-367-6640

duck

Millennium Trail

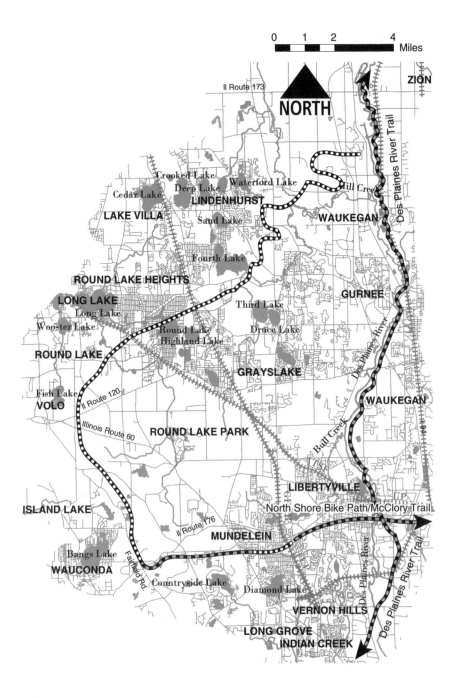

Millennium Trail Bike Path
Hawley Street Section

Extending eastward from the Lakewood Millennium Trail is the Millennium Trail Bike Path. This additional 3 mile section is asphalt paved and parallels the south side of Hawley Street to Chevy Chase Road, then continues on the north side Hawley Street to Midlothian Road where it currently ends. There is a traffic signal at Chevy Chase Road. It will eventually be extended another 1.7 miles where it will connect to the North Shore Bike Path.

For more information:
Lake County Division of Transportation
847-362-3750

rabbit baby

Millennium Trail Bike Path
Hawley Street Section

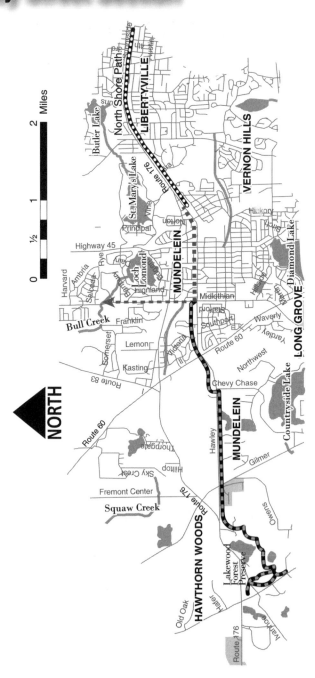

North Shore Path

The 8 mile long North Shore Path, built on the abandoned North Shore Rail Line, parallels the south side of Route 176 west from Lake Bluff, through Libertyville, to Brice Street in Mundelein. You can find parking on the nearby streets in downtown Lake Bluff just east of Sheridan Road. The trail surface is asphalt from Lake Bluff to Waukegan Road. The remaining surface to Brice Street is crushed limestone, except for a short stretch before Milwaukee Avenue.

Starting out from Lake Bluff, the trail begins where it connects to the Robert McClory Bike Path, just south of the Route 176 bridge overpass. There are actually two intersection points. The one closest to the overpass takes you down a short dip with curves before it flattens out. The other access, a couple hundred feet further south, is more gradual. Once you pass through a short section of dense woods, you will enter into a setting of open and light industry on your left with Route 176 to your right. A half mile into the ride, there is an underpass to get you across Green Bay Road. For a side trip, there is an .8 mile asphalt path that will take you north from Route 176, past the Lake Bluff community pool and golf course, to

North Shore Path

the Lake Bluff city limits where it ends. Once past Waukegan Road the setting is more forest like to your left (south) and business/industrial on your right.

Three miles into the ride you'll come to Lamb's Farm, just east of I-94. Lamb's Farm is a non-profit training center and residence for the mentally handicapped. Here you will find parking, a children's farmyard, miniature golf, country store, an ice cream stand and a restaurant. Festivals and special events are held here year round.

There is an underpass at the I-94 tollway, but at St. Mary's Road, the street crossing is at the traffic light. As you approach the Jamaican Gardens Nursery, you will see a narrow dirt path on your left. This is one of the connections to the Des Plaines River Trail. The paved connection is on the east side of the Des Plaines River, a little further on.

At Milwaukee Avenue and again at Butterfield Road, a mile further, you must go to the traffic light to cross. The ride through Libertyville is residential with several street crossings. From Butterfield Road to Brice Street, the trail is tree lined and quiet. Shortly before the end of the ride at you will pass Mt. Carmel High School, with a large parking area, on your left. To the north of Route 176 is the Marytown/Saint Maximilian Shrine, operated by the Franciscan Friars. Here you can tour its beautiful grounds, visit the historic shrine and browse through the gift shop. Adjoining Marytown to the west is St. Mary of the Lake Seminary.

Getting there:

To get to the Lake Bluff trailhead take Route 176 past the Sheridan Road over pass and curve to the left. This takes you immediately to the Lake Bluff shopping area, and the Lake Bluff train station across Sheridan Road. There is parking in downtown Lake Bluff near the train station, at Sheridan Road and Scranton. There is no off street parking on Brice Street.

For more information:

Lake County Division of Transportation
847-362-3950

North Shore Path

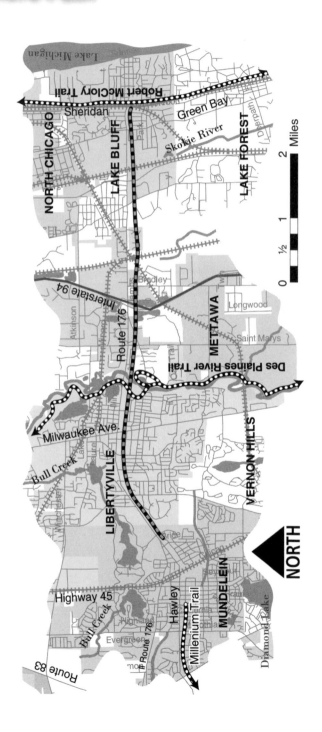

Old School Forest Preserve

This 380 acre Preserve is located in south-central Lake County, near Libertyville. Old School was the first Forest Preserve in Illinois to blend native prairie restoration with recreational facilities. Small prairies are interspersed among the large oaks that dominate the woodlands in this area.

A 3 mile crushed-gravel loop explores Old School's woods and prairies and is open to hikers, bicyclists, horseback riders and cross-country skiers. A portion of this loop is part of the Des Plaines River Trail (DPRT). A 1.5 mile crushed-gravel loop encircles the lake and is open to hikers, bicyclists and cross-country skiers. The

Old School Forest Preserve

1.5 mile asphalt road winding through the Preserve offers a special one-way lane popular with bicyclists and in-line skaters. Old School's sled hill is one of the most popular features of this Preserve and can be seen from the Interstate 94 Tollway.

The DPRT winds through this Preserve and is open to hikers, bicyclists, horseback riders and cross-country skiers.

There are five picnic shelters, two of which have lookout towers. All offer drinking water, comfort stations and cooking grills. Permits are required for picnic shelters. The Preserve also provides a playground for the youngsters and a popular sled hill. Call the Forest Preserves' Winter Sports Hotline at 847-968-3235 for conditions.

Getting there:

The main entrance is on St. Mary's Road, one-half mile south of Route 176. St. Mary's Road runs north and south, and is west of the I-94 Tollway and east of Milwaukee Avenue (Route 21). There is also access by foot or bike from the North Shore Bike Path just east of the Des Plaines River. The North Shore Path runs parallel to the south side of Route 176. Open hours are 6:30 a.m. to sunset.

frog

For more information:

Lake County Forest Preserves
www.LCFPD.org
2000 North Milwaukee Avenue
Libertyville, Illinois 60048
847-367-6640

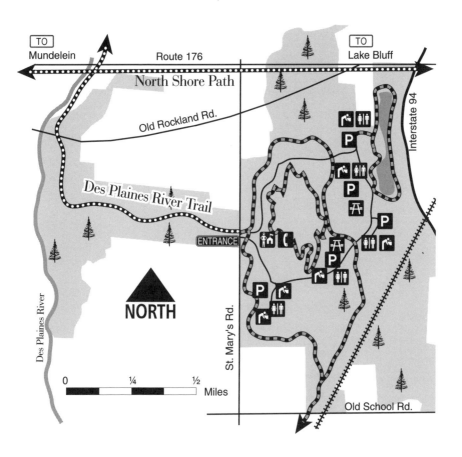

Robert McClory Bike Path

The Robert McClory Bike Path is built on the Lake County portion of the abandoned Chicago North Shore Milwaukee Railway right-of-way. The path runs for 25 miles from the Cook County line at Lake Cook Road to the Wisconsin border. South of the Lake County line the trail continues as the Green Bay Trail into Kenilworth. North of Lake County into Wisconsin it continues as the Kenosha County Trail. It also connects to the North Shore Trail in Lake Bluff and the Zion Bike Path. The trail generally parallels the east side of Green Bay Road and the west side of Sheridan Road.

The mostly urban to suburban setting of this ride provides ample opportunities to enjoy the many eating establishments and beautiful homes. It's open to bicycling, hiker/joggers, in-line skaters and cross-country skiing. Between Cook County and Lake Bluff, the trail is limestone screening to Highland Park and paved north of Highwood to Lake Bluff's city limits. North of Lake Bluff to Wisconsin the surface is mostly limestone screenings except for a 1 mile concrete sidewalk section in North Chicago and a 1.5 mile asphalt paved section that forms the west side of the Zion Bike Path loop.

The Robert McClory trail officially begins northbound from Lake Cook Road, a little east of Green Bay Road, by the Braeside train station. The surface here is crushed gravel. A mile north of this point there you'll come to the Ravinia train station, with restaurants nearby. There is parking at the Ravinia Festival Park south lot on St. John's Avenue in Highland Park. Note that cars left after 4 p.m. in the summer during the concert season will be ticketed. For a short side trip go to Rosewood Beach Park with its scenic view on a high bluff overlooking Lake Michigan. To get there head east on Roger Williams Avenue for ¾ miles, past Jens Jensen Park.

There are several sidewalk & street connections as you proceed north through Highland Park and Highwood. The off-road temporarily ends at the Highland Park train station at the intersection of St. John's and Laurel Avenues. To continue north, take St. John's one block north to Central Avenue. Turn east (right) a block to Sheridan Road. Turn north (left) on Sheridan pass Moraine Park, where you'll find drinking water, restrooms, and a picnic area. Pick up Sheridan Road again by following the signs north into Highwood by way of Edgecliff Drive, Oak Street, and Walker Avenue. You'll pass Fort Sheridan on the east. Continue north along Sheridan Road to the Fort Sheridan train station at the intersection of Old Elm road and Sheridan Road north of Highwood, where the trail picks up again, and is asphalt surfaced. The distance of this described trail gap is about 3 miles.

As you continue north into Lake Forest, you pass DePaul's University Barat College and through the downtown area. Here there are a number of good restaurants, an ice cream shop and many shopping opportunities. Market Square, built in 1916, was the first shopping area in the County. If you turn east (right) on Deerpath Road for 1 mile, it will take you to Forest Park and the scenic bluffs overlooking Lake Michigan. There are bike

Robert McClory Bike Path

racks by the stairs to the beach, and a long elevated boardwalk that winds through the trees to the shoreline.

There are two intersections on the trail before you cross over the bridge to the Lake Bluff train station. The Robert McClory Path continues north. The two westbound intersections take you on the North Shore Path, which parallels the south side of Route 176. There is parking in downtown Lake Bluff near the train station, at Sheridan Road and Scranton. From the train station, the trees provide a canopy of shade during the summer.

In North Chicago you pass the Great Lakes Naval Training Center on the right, and you'll come to another street connection. At Martin Luther King Drive (22nd Street), go west one block to Commonwealth, then north a block to Broadway. A short distance to the right you pick up the trail again at Boak Park, just west of Glen. There are many street crossings as you proceed through North Chicago and Waukegan. You can park your car on one of the side streets near the Lake County YMCA on Golf Avenue for easy trail access in Waukegan. From Golf Avenue for the 3.5 miles to Zion there are only three street crossings. The setting in this stretch is quiet and suburban, with scrub growth and low trees lining the trail.

As you enter Zion, the trail is paved. Just north of 21st Street the crushed gravel path resumes at the trail intersection. Stay left as the Zion Bike Path goes to the right. For a detour to the Illinois Beach State Park, go east on Carmel Blvd at the southwest corner of the Zion Bike Path for a mile to Sheridan Road. Cross Sheridan Road, looping north to Shiloh Blvd. Just past Shiloh is a path leading to the Northern Unit of the Illinois Beach State Park.

North of Zion the setting becomes more rural, with woods with meadows bordering the trail. As you cross into Wisconsin past the Russell Road overpass, the path continues for another 3.5 miles as the Kenosha County Bike Trail. The setting along this stretch is mostly rural. At 89th Street the off-road trail ends. There is a convenient place to rest across the street at Anderson Park.

If you decide to continue on and explore Kenosha's parks and the harbor along Lake Michigan, take 89th Street east to 17th Avenue, then south to 91st Street. Go East on 91st Street to 7th Avenue, then north to Southport Park. Sightseeing as you continue north includes the Third Avenue Historic District. This is Kenosha's 'mansion' district with many large period revival homes. Further north is Eichelman Park, which has a bathing beach, and Kenosha Marina, a large boat slip marina with entertainment and recreation facilities.

Backtracking to where we started at Lake Cook Road, you can take the connecting 6 mile, paved Green Bay Trail south to Forest Avenue in Kenilworth where it ends. One way to get from there to the Chicago Lakefront Bike Path is to take Forest Avenue east to Sheridan Road, then Sheridan Road south to Lincoln Avenue in Evanston. You'll find the Lakefront Path trailhead east of Sheridan Road off Lincoln Avenue.

Getting there:

There are multiple accesses to the path throughout the length of the path. Some of the locations for off street parking are described above.

For more information:

Lake County Division of Transportation
847-362-3950

Robert McClory Bike Path

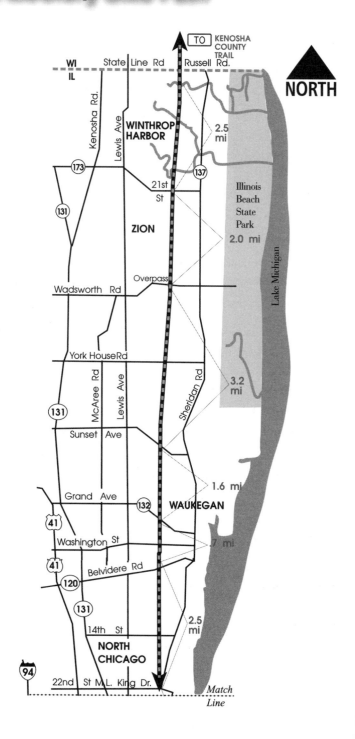

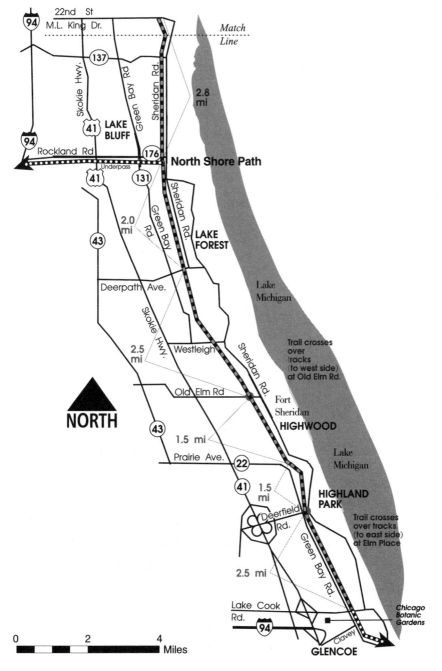

22nd St
M.L. King Dr.
94

137

Skokie Hwy.
Green Bay Rd
Sheridan Rd.

2.8 mi

41 **LAKE BLUFF**

94
Rockland Rd
Underpass
176 **North Shore Path**

41
131

Sheridan Rd.
Green Bay Rd.

2.0 mi

43

LAKE FOREST

Deerpath Ave.

Lake Michigan

Skokie Hwy.

2.5 mi

Westleigh

Sheridan Rd.

Trail crosses
over
tracks
(to west side)
at Old Elm Rd.

Old Elm Rd

▲ **NORTH**

43

Fort Sheridan
HIGHWOOD

1.5 mi

Prairie Ave.
22

Lake Michigan

41
1.5 mi

HIGHLAND PARK

Deerfield Rd.

Trail crosses
over tracks
(to east side)
at Elm Place

Green Bay Rd.

2.5 mi

Lake Cook Rd.
94

Chicago Botanic Gardens

Clavey
GLENCOE

0   2   4 Miles

117

Rollins Savanna Forest Preserve

At the time of this publication Rollins Savanna is closed for trail development and the addition of public access facilities. Anticipated opening is sometime in 2004. Updates will be available at the LCFP website. This is the second largest Forest Preserve in Lake County with 1,225 acres.

The Preserve is located in north central Lake County near Grayslake. It contains scattered groves of majestic oaks, wide-open prairies teeming with wildflowers, native grasses and abundant wetlands.

When open, the Preserve will offer over 5.7 miles of gravel trail with bridges and boardwalks for hiking, biking, and nature and wildlife observation. It will consist of a 5 mile, 12 foot-wide gravel trail encircling a large open area, providing views of both upland and wetland wildlife habitat area. There is also a .7 mile, 8 foot-wide gravel educational trail loop planned to provide for educational programs for local schools and the College of Lake County. Snowmobiles will be able to parallel a small section of the trail as they pass through the Preserve.

Improvements will include an 80-car parking lot off Washington Street, restrooms, trailside nature education exhibits and observation blinds. Secondary Preserve access and a 40-car parking area will be available on Drury Lane along with access to 1.5 miles of additional gravel trail, which will be part of the planned Millennium Trail. Plans also include a nature seed area with greenhouse and a wildlife observation area.

Getting there:

The main entrance will be off Washington Street across from Atkinson Road, about .2 miles east of Route 83 and 1.4 miles west of Route 45. The preserve is open from 6:30 a.m. to sunset.

For more information:

Lake County Forest Preserves
www.LCFPD.org (updates will be available on line)
2000 North Milwaukee Avenue
Libertyville, Illinois 60048
847-367-6640

Photo courtesy of Lake County Forest Preserves and Keith J. Portman © 2003

Rollins Savanna Forest Preserve

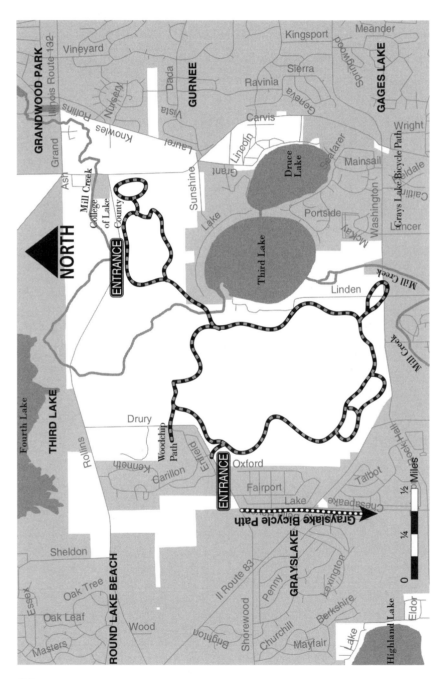

Ryerson Conservation Area

The 552 acre Ryerson Conservation Area is located near Deerfield in southeastern Lake County. It is home to the environmental education center for the Lake County Forest Preserves.

Ryerson Woods is one of the best examples of a northern flatwoods forest, a rare northern Illinois landscape. The Preserve supports some of Illinois' most pristine woodlands and several state threatened and endangered species, and offers 6.5 miles of scenic trails that wind through a stately forest to the quiet Des Plaines River. Because it is a nature preserve and environmental education center, trails are open to hikers, and when snow is at least 4 inches deep, cross-country skiers. Bicycles, snowmobiles, dogs, horses and other pets are not allowed.

Programs are offered year-round for families, adults, children, teachers and community groups. Also, dozens of guided and self-guided programs are available to school and youth groups. At the small farm area, you may spot cows, sheep, goats, pigs, chickens and turkeys. Don't miss the butterfly garden in summer, located near the Visitors Center. Spring is the time for wildflowers and autumn is show time in the maple forest.

Ryerson Conservation Area

Getting there:

The entrance is on Riverwoods Road, 1.5 miles south of Half Day Road (Route 22) and 2 miles north of Deerfield Road, just west of the I-94 Tollway. Open hours are 6:30 a.m. to sunset.

For more information:

Lake County Forest Preserves
www.LCFPD.org
2000 North Milwaukee Avenue
Libertyville, Illinois 60048
847-367-6640

sparrow hawk

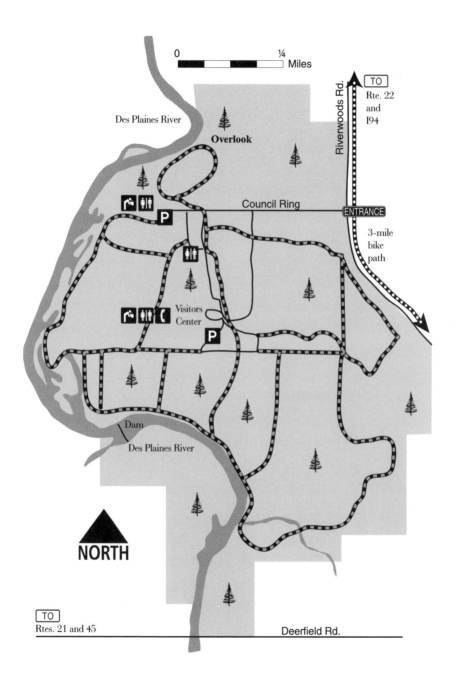

0 ¼ Miles

Des Plaines River

Overlook

Riverwoods Rd.

TO
Rte. 22
and
I94

Council Ring

ENTRANCE

3-mile
bike
path

P

Visitors
Center

P

Dam

Des Plaines River

NORTH

TO
Rtes. 21 and 45

Deerfield Rd.

123

Skokie Valley Trail

The Skokie Valley Trial is built on a converted railroad right-of-way. It parallels the west side of Hwy 41 northbound from West Park in Highland Park. Just before Route 60 it crosses over Hwy 41 as it continues on the eastside north to Laurel Avenue in Lake Forest. There are about 50 feet of scrub and tree growth separating the trail from the Highway. The total distance is 6.5 miles. The surface is asphalt and is in good condition. There was considerable activity on the trail during my visit with bikers, in-line skaters or joggers always in view.

Getting there:

There is no designated parking along the path, and street parking along the cross streets is limited and often not conveniently available.

For more information:

Lake County Division of Transportation
847-362-3950

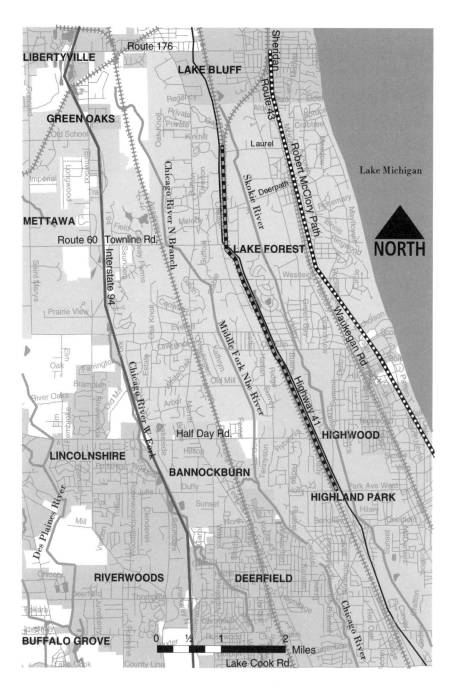

Van Patten Woods Forest Preserve & Sterling Lake

Van Patten Woods is located in northeastern Lake County near Wadsworth. The 991 acre Preserve is one of the premier recreation sites in Lake County. A majestic oak forest, 74 acre Sterling Lake, and the Des Plaines River provide a picturesque backdrop for outdoor recreation activities such as fishing, picnicking, horseback riding and flying model aircraft.

The Des Plaines River Trail bisects the Preserve and is open to horses, bicycles, snowmobiles, and hikers. Its trailhead is at the far northern Russell Road entrance. It can also be accessed from other trails with the Preserve.

Five mile of crushed granite trails offer fun for hikers, bicyclists, cross-country skiers and horseback riders. On the Preserve's eastern half are two trails: a 1 mile loop for hikers and cross-county skiers, and a 2 mile loop for hikers, bikers, cross-country skiers and horseback riders. There are two additional trails in the eastern half: a 1 mile loop for hikers and cross-country skiers, and a 2 mile crushed gravel loop available for multi-use.

Sterling Lake is the center of activity here. This formal gravel quarry has two basins, each encircled by a 1 mile gravel trail. Bicycles, canoes, rowboats, and fishing equipment can be rented at Chandlers' Boat and Bait Shop (847-526-8217). See the adjoining map for location.

Van Patten Woods also hosts a rustic tent youth campground, model aircraft field, a playground and a sports field. Drinking water, comfort stations, picnic tables, shelters and parking areas are located throughout the Preserve. Permits are required for horseback riding, the picnic shelters, youth campground and the model aircraft field.

The predominant natural features of the Preserve are the Des Plaines River and its adjacent floodplain, which provide flood control to Lake County and serves as a refuge to native species. On the higher elevation to the river's east are native oak woodlands and planted pine groves. Van Patten Woods was created in 1961, and was Lake County's first Forest Preserve.

Getting there:

The main entrance is on Route 173, one mile east of the I-94 Tollway and a ¼ mile east of Route 41. Another trailhead, with horse trailer parking, is on the south side of Russell Road, ¾ miles east of Route 41. Just east of there, on the north side of Russell Road is the entrance to the Youth Campground and the Model Aircraft Field. The preserve is open from 6: 30 a.m. to sunset.

For more information:

Lake County Forest Preserves
www.LCFPD.org
2000 North Milwaukee Avenue
Libertyville, Illinois 60048
(847) 367-6640

Van Patten Woods Forest Preserve & Sterling Lake

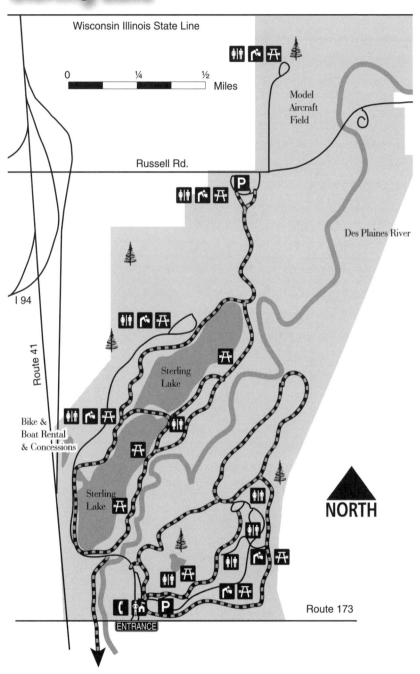

Wisconsin Illinois State Line

0   ¼   ½
Miles

Model Aircraft Field

Russell Rd.

Des Plaines River

I 94

Route 41

Sterling Lake

Bike & Boat Rental & Concessions

Sterling Lake

NORTH

Route 173

ENTRANCE

Vernon Hills Trails

Vernon Hills offers 7 miles of asphalt paved hiking and biking trails connecting its parks and the Des Plaines River Trail.

The 2.9 mile path north of Route 60 takes you into Century Park and parking. It loops around Little Bear and Big Bear Lakes, through open fields, woods, across bridges, past exercise stations and into neighborhoods of residences and apartments. Park facilities include concessions, restrooms, picnic tables, a sledding hill, and playground equipment.

South of Route 60 the trail takes you along Lakeview Parkway to Deerpath and Marimac Parks. There is a pedestrian button at the stoplight for crossing over Route 60. Once on the south side of Route 60 turn west (right) at Phillip Road. Continue south .75 miles of Route 60 to Deerpath Park. Here you'll pass by tennis courts, ball fields and a playground. From there the path runs along Seavey Creek to Marimac Park, extending into residential areas to Route 45. It continues on the north side of Route 45 to its end at Clinton Road.

The path east (left) along Lakeview Parkway takes you to the Canoe Launch and the Des Plaines River Trail. It loops around Freeway Drive and Bunker Court through

Vernon Hills Trails

an executive park When you get to Milwaukee Avenue (Route 21), turn north (left), and cross over Route 21 at the first stoplight. Continue east through the Rivertree Court shopping center. At the stop sign turn left. The pathway along Route 60 connects with the Des Plaines River Trail at the canoe launch area.

Getting there:

From Milwaukee Avenue (Route 21) take Route 60 west .75 miles to Lakeview Parkway. Turn north (right), then left for a half mile into Century Park. To get to Deerpath Park, continue on Route 60 a .25 mile past Lakeview Parkway. Go south on Deerpath until you come to Cherokee Road. Deerpath Park is on the left.

For more information:

Vernon Hills Park District
847-367-7270

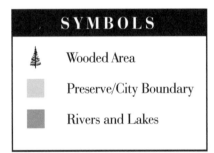

SYMBOLS

🌲 Wooded Area

☐ Preserve/City Boundary

▨ Rivers and Lakes

LEGEND

▪▪▪▪▪▪▪ Hiking/Biking Trail
- - - - - - Hiking only Trail
▫▫▫▫▫▫ Alternate Trail
•••••••••• Horseback/Snowmobile Trail
- - - - - - Planned Trail
++++++++++ Railroad Tracks

Facilities

🔺 Camping
➕ First Aid
🍴 Food/Concession
ℹ Information
🛏 Lodging
🅿 Parking
🎪 Picnic Area
🧍 Rangers Station
🚻 Restroom
🏠 Shelter
☎ Telephone
🚰 Water

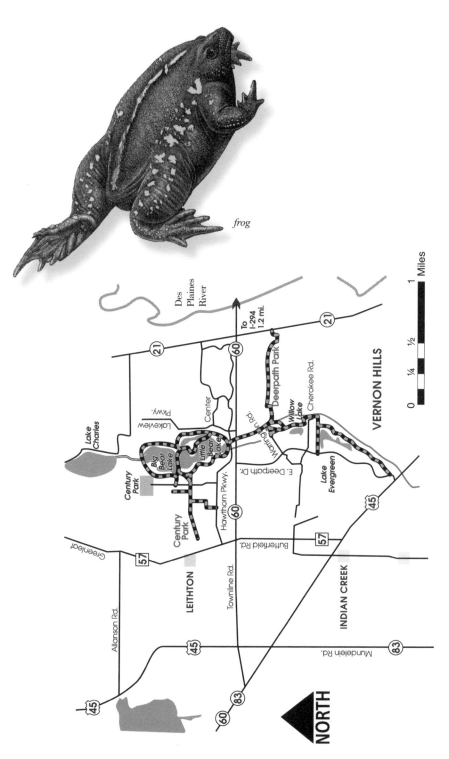

frog

131

Volo Bog State Natural Area

Volo Bog is a 1,200 acre nature area in northwest Lake County, near Ingleside and south of Fox Lake. It contains one of the rarest ecosystems in Illinois.

The current landscape was shaped mainly by glacial activity, with marshes, woodlands, prairies, and the bog as its center point. As the glacier began to melt thousands of years ago, it deposited a blanket of debris, collective called glacial till, which includes clay, sand, gravel and boulders.

The Bog was originally a deep 50 acre lake with poor drainage that began filling with vegetation about 6,000 years ago. As these plants died and decomposed, the peat mat thickened, forming a floating mat of sphagnum, moss, cattails and sedges surrounding an open pool of water in the center.

The Volo Bog Interpretive Trial, for hikers only, is a ½ mile loop leading visitors through each state of bog succession. The path consists of woodchips, with wooden dock sections and boardwalks.

Tamarack View Trail is a 2.75 mile trail open to hiking and cross-country skiing. Here you pass through woods, wetlands, fields and prairie. There are also two one mile connecting trail loops (Deerpath and Prairie Ridge Loops) that have been added for those wishing to venture further. The higher elevations along the trail provide views of the Volo Bog basin and the tamarack trees. The trailhead can be found just south of the visitor center and it moves in a counter clockwise direction.

Volo Bog supports a great variety of songbirds, waterfowl and wading birds that stop by as they migrate north to their nesting areas. Summer brings forth the orchids, and the delicate grass pin and rose pogonia. Whitetail deer, mink, muskrat, raccoon, sandhill cranes, great blue and green-backed herons occupy this natural area.

The Visitor Center is housed in a dairy barn. It includes a program room, the Tamarack Shop, exhibits, discovery area, reference library and restrooms. Volunteer naturalists lead one-hour public tours on Saturdays and Sundays at 11:00 a.m. and 1:00 p.m. Volunteers also assist with youth and adult group programs. There is a picnic area and privy located adjacent to the parking lot.

Getting there:

From Route 12 take Brandenburg Road west for 1.2 mile to the entrance on the south side of the road.

For more information:

Volo Bog State Natural Area
28478 W. Brandenburg Road
Ingleside, Illinois 60041
815-344-1294

Volo Bog State Natural Area

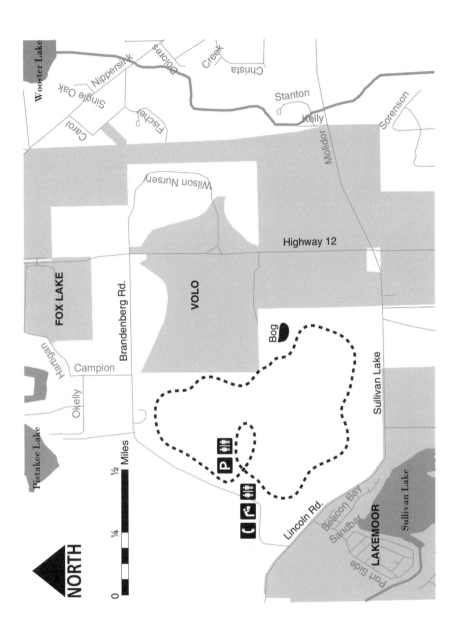

Walter Heller Nature Center

This 97 acre interpretive center and nature park is located in Highland Park, in southeast Lake County.

Here you will be able to enjoy 3.3 miles of crushed gravel and woodchip trail open to hiking and cross-country skiing. The trail system is mostly a series of interconnecting loops, and is open from dawn to dusk. The Red Trail takes you through a canopied pine forest. The Blue Trail leads one through a hardwood forest and to a small pond.

The Interpretive Center provides a Discovery Room, and offers youth summer camps, many nature and environmental programs. There is a flourishing prairie nearby. Restrooms, drinking water, telephone and a picnic area are available.

Getting there:

The Park is located north of Route 22 and south of Old Elm Road. Exit Route 41 eastbound on Half Day Road (Route 22), to the entrance on the west side of the road.

For more information:

Heller Nature Center • Park District of Highland Park
2821 Ridge Road
Highland Park, Illinois 60035
847-433-6901

Walter Heller Nature Center

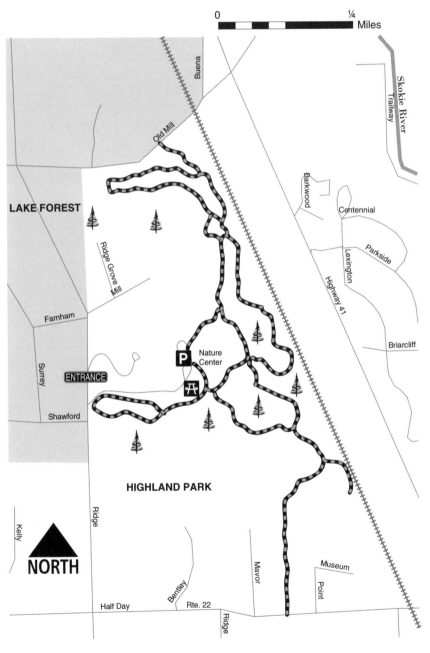

0 ¼ Miles

Skokie River
Trailway

Buena

Old Mill

LAKE FOREST

Barkwood

Centennial

Ridge Grove Mill

Lexington

Parkside

Highway 41

Farnham

P Nature Center

Briarcliff

Surrey

ENTRANCE

Shawford

HIGHLAND PARK

Kelly

Ridge

NORTH

Mavor

Museum

Point

Bentley

Half Day

Rte. 22

Ridge

Zion's Bike Path

Zion is located in northeast Lake County. The city has 6.5 miles of asphalt surfaced trail, of which 2.3 miles is bikeway on streets and the reminder off road. This is a loop trail with the west side running north from Carmel Blvd. along Galilee Avenue. This section also serves as a part of the Robert McClory Bike Path. At 18th Street, the trail turns east running along the south side of Beulah Park, connecting to 17th Street. Continue on 17th Street across Sheridan Road to Hillside Avenue, where the trail turns south just west of the railroad tracks. Proceed south to Carmel Blvd. and turn west. At Sheridan Road, go south one block to 33rd Street, and then north after a block on Elisha Avenue where you pick up Carmel Blvd. going west to complete your ride. A leg of the path follows the north side of Shiloh Blvd. from the tracks to a small parking area just west of the Zion Power Plant. From there you can access the north section of the Illinois Beach State Park trail. There is a short path running northeast from the parking area that will take you to Zion Park District's 'Hosah Park Preservation Area'. Its boardwalks are built over dunes and will provide you a scenic view of Lake Michigan and the surrounding landscape.

Zion's Bike Path

Getting there:

Take Sheridan Road (Route 173) to Zion. Parking is available along most of the route and throughout the community.

For more information:

Zion Park District
2400 Dowie Memorial Drive
Zion, Illinois 60099
847-746-5500

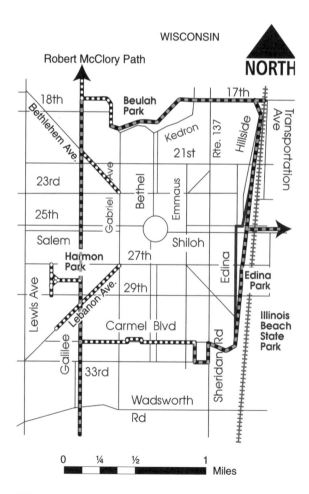

Photo courtesy of Lake County Forest Preserves and Keith J. Portman © 2003

Events & Programs

Lake County Forest Preserves

You should refer to the website at www. LCFPD.org for their calendar of current events as they are subject to change, or call 847-367-6640 and request a free copy of the Horizons newsletter. Some program fees apply and registration may be required. The following listing notes many of the popular programs that have been available.

Entertainment

Independence Grove – The Millennia Plaza serves as a natural amphitheater and provides a striking backdrop for enjoyable evenings of music and special performances. Located on Buckley Road (route 137) just east of Milwaukee Avenue (Route 21) near Libertyville.

Greenbelt Cultural Center – Family entertainment featuring an outstanding line up of great performances that offer something for everyone. Bring a lawn chair or blanket and umbrella (for shade). The Greenbelt Cultural Center is located on the east side of Green Bay Road, south of Belvidere Road (Route 120) near North Chicago and Waukegan.

Fun For All

Stargazing - Join the Skokie Valley Astronomers for indoor programs followed (on clear nights) by stargazing with club telescopes. Free. Call 630-393-7929

Night Bike Ride - Experience the unique sights and sounds of nature at night as you ride your bikes on the Des Plaines River Trail. Helmet and bike light are required.

Voyageurs of Little Fort - Take a trip in a giant canoe from the past. Paddle the lake while learning about Lake County's fur trade in 1740 and the lives of the voyageurs.

A Walk Among the Wildflowers – Uncover the secrets of wildflowers. Discover the folklore, superstitions and healing powers they hold.

Explore a Forest Preserve after dark – A short hike and fun activities to discover a few of the special adaptations that allow some animals to be active at night.

Maple Syruping One hour hikes. Learn why the trees have sweet sap and how to tell which trees to tap.

Outdoor Adventures

Canoeing the Summer Solstice – Learn about the fact and legends of the longest day of sunlight. Equipment provided. Difficulty easy.

Learn to Canoe I & II - Perfect nine strokes and five maneuvers as you paddle with ease and confidence through their obstacle course. Moderate physical difficulty.

Learn to Kayak - Participants will be introduced to basic paddling safety issues, using double-bladed paddles, launching and landing techniques, and efficient forward, back, and turning strokes. Strenuous physical difficulty.

Earthfest – Greenbelt Cultural Center. Celebrate Earth Day with games, wagon rides and crafts. Discover the "Wonders of our Wetlands" in hands-on activities.

Photography

Nature Photography – Join the Riverwoods Nature Photographic Society for its varied programs. Adults only. There is a fee, but no registration required. 847-945-3909

Events & Programs (continued)

Bats - Discover their feeding and roosting habitats, reproductive strategies, migratory and hibernation behavior, and their importance in the ecosystem. Then watch their emergence at dusk.

Wetlands of Lake County – Walks that focus on the importance and formation of different types of wetlands, and identification of characteristic plants and animals in each. Led by naturalists from the US Fish and Wildlife Service, the Illinois Dept. of Natural Resources and the Forest Preserve.

Ferns, Horsetails and Club Mosses - A two-part primer course first consisting of a lab session where you will learn fern identification skills through a slide presentation, pressed specimens, and ecology field notes. The field trip session will take participants to one of the most fern-rich habitats in Lake County, where you will learn ferns and their allies in their natural settings.

Tree ID – Learn various identifying features, terminology, and how to use a key to identify broadleaf trees on your own. Find out where to expect to find particular kinds of trees growing by identifying natural communities.

Butterfly Gardening - Learn how gardeners can help foster these winged jewels. A slide presentation will reveal the secrets of designing your own butterfly garden and which plants are best to attract them to your yard.

Landscaping for Wildlife - Discover the benefits to using native plants in your landscape plan. Discussion includes plant selection and identification, habitat requirements and maintenance as you tour the Native Plant Garden.

Lake County Birding 101 – An in-depth look at the waterfowl and warbler segments of Lake County's bird population. Each two-part class includes an evening classroom session and a Saturday field trip

Workshops

Bird banding: Research in Action – Become an integral part of an ongoing research project that collects data about bird migration through banding. Watch skillful bird handling, help collect data and get a view of colorful spring migrants.

Building a Backyard for Birds – Learn what it takes to get birds to live in your backyard. Enhance the beauty of any yard while increasing its attractiveness to birds.

Youth Programs

Knee High Naturalists (Spring; Summer day camp) – Discover nature through your child's eyes as you explore a preserve with a naturalist.

Youth Night Hikes – Nocturnal lifestyles, camouflage and night vision will be explored. Each section is different.

Winter Day Camp - Topics include birds, mammals, trees, tracks, signs, insulation, territory, food and shelter.

Organizations

Bicycling
Bicycle Club of Lake County   847-265-6235
PO Box 521
Libertyville, IL 60048

Bicycling (continued)

Chicagoland Bicycle Federation   312-427-3325
650 S. Clark Street
Chicago, IL 60605

Wheeling Wheelmen   847-520-5010
PO Box 7304
Wheeling, IL 60089

Hiking

American Hiking Society   301-565-6704
1422 Fenwick Lane
Silver Springs, MD 20910

Environmental

Lake County Forest Preserves   847-367-6640
2000 North Milwaukee Avenue
Libertyville, Illinois 60048

Illinois Trails Conservancy   815-735-8137
PO Box 10
Capron, IL 62012

Friends of Ryerson Woods   847-965-3321
Ryerson Conservation Area
21950 North Riverwoods Road
Deerfield, IL 60015

Friends of Heller   847-433-6901
Heller Nature Center
636 Ridge Road
Highland park, IL 60035

Illinois Dunesland Preservation Society   847-746-1090
PO box 466
Zion, IL 60099

Lake Forest Open Lands Association   847-234-3880
272 East Deerpath
Lake Forest, IL 60045

Lake Bluff Open Lands Association   847-735-8137
325 East Scranton Avenue
Lake Bluff, IL 60044

Nature Conservancy, Illinois Chapter   312-580-2100
8 South Michigan Avenue
Chicago, IL 60603

Friends of Volo Bog   815-344-1294
28478 West Brandenburg Road
Ingleside, IL 60041

Photography
Riverwoods Nature Photographic Society   630-393-7929
Ryerson Conservation Area
21950 North Riverwoods Road
Deerfield, IL 60015

Lake County's Bicycle Stores

Check at your local bicycle or book store for additional copies of this
book and other Hiking and Biking publications.

Antioch Schwinn Cyclery   Buffalo Grove Cycling & Fitness
890 Main Street   960 S. Buffalo Grove Road
Antioch, IL 60002   Buffalo Grove, IL 60089
847-395-6500   847-541-4670

Bikes Plus   Deerfield Schwinn
203 W Northwest Hwy   705 Waukegan Road
Barrington, IL 60010   Deerfield, IL 60015
847-382-9200   847-945-0700

Tailwinds Cyclery
1816 Belvidere Road
Grayslake, IL 60030
847-223-1798

Grayslake Bicycle Shop & Repair
140 Center Street
Grayslake, IL 60030
847-543-4756

Mike's Bikes of Gurnee
4641 Old Grand Avenue
Gurnee, IL 60031
847-662-8482

Higher Gear
1874 Sheridan Road
Highland Park, IL 60035
847-433-2453

North Shore Bicycles
790 Sheridan Road
Highwood, IL 60040
847-432-1369

R R B Cycles
562 Green Bay road
Kenilworth, IL 60043
847-251-7878

Kiddles Bike & Sport
258 Market Square
Lake Forest, IL 60045
847-234-0025

The Cyclery
575 Ela Road
Lake Zurich, IL 60047
847-438-9600

Higher Gear
2105 E Grand Avenue
Lindenhurst, IL 60046
847-265-8230

Libertyville Cyclery
800 N Milwaukee Avenue
Libertyville, IL 60048
847-362-6030

Chris Cycle Center
130 Peterson Road
Libertyville, IL 60048
847-680-9622

Shamrock Cyclery
344 Old McHenry Road
Long Grove, IL 60047
847-013-9767

M & M Cyclery
337 N Seymour Avenue
Mundelein, IL 60060
847-566-2453

B & G Cyclery
131 E Rollins Road
Round Lake, IL 60073
847-740-0007

Pacific Bicycles
100 N. Fairway Dr.
Vernon Hills, IL 60061
847-573-0686

Midwest Bicycle & Billiard
1928 Grand Avenue
Waukegan, IL 60085
847-249-5670

Waukegan Schwinn
75 S. Green Bay Road
Waukegan, IL 60085
847-336-3432

Zion Schwinn Cyclery
2750 Sheridan Road
Zion, IL 60099
847-746-2200

Find me a place, safe and serene,

away from the terror I see on the screen.

A place where my soul can find some peace,

away from the stress and the pressures released.

A corridor of green not far from my home

for fresh air and exercise, quiet will roam.

Summer has smells that tickle my nose

and fall has the leaves that crunch under my toes.

Beware, comes a person we pass in a while

with a wave and hello and a wide friendly smile.

Recreation trails are the place to be,

to find that safe haven of peace and serenity.

By Beverly Moore, Illinois Trails Conservancy

American Bike Trails publishes and distributes
maps, books and guides for the bicyclist.
For more information:

American Bike Trails
610 Hillside Avenue
Antioch, IL 60002
800-246-4627
w w w . a b t r a i l s . c o m

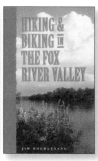

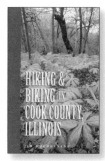